PABLO ANTONIO CUADRA

BOOK OF HOURS

ENGLISH TRANSLATION: SARAH HORNSBY
AND MATTHEW C. HORNSBY

Managua, Nicaragua, 2012
Academia Nicaragüense de la Lengua

4

Edition of the Academia Nicaragüense de la Lengua

Editorial Counsel:
Jorge Eduardo Arellano, Francisco Arellano Oviedo, Sergio
Ramírez Mercado, Rosario Fiallos de Aguilar, Isolda Rodríguez
Rosales, Julio Valle-Castillo, Pedro Xavier Solís.

Title: *Book of Hours*

English Translation: Sarah Hornsby
and Matthew C. Hornsby

Proof-reading:
Horacio Peña

Coordination:
Francisco Arellano Oviedo

Layout:
Lydia González Martinica. PAVSA.

Cover Design:
Francisco Arellano Jr. PAVSA

Cover illustration:
Nohelia Talavera

Internal Illustrations:
Nohelia Talavera: 14, 46, 50, 64, 72, 105, 122, 149, 278, 292
Matthew C. Hornsby: 48, 106, 108, 115, 125, 150
Sarah Hornsby: 126 (from a petroglyph in Chaquitillo, Matagalpa.)
PAC: 157, 165, 172, 179, 191, 201, 211, 221, 229, 247, 259, 267, 314
Thomas Merton: 308

Managua, Nicaragua, November 2012
© Academia Nicaragüense de la Lengua

Dedication

For those who come and go
        and come again
for those who love Nicaragua
        then hate, then love more
for those who love Jesus
        and would see Him in his
        people of Nicaragua
for those who are seeking truth
        but have not yet found a name
        for it
        PAC is a true guide.

Appreciation

To Lorraine Stuart for encouragement.

Table of Contents

8

THE ROUND OF THE YEAR

FOREWORD

by Pedro Xavier Solis Cuadra

My grandfather, Pablo Antonio Cuadra, had a Biblical father: full of history, patriarchal, cattle rancher and with an immense library. My great-grandfather, Carlos Cuadra Pasos, gifted more than a century to the childhood of my grandfather. And there in those books this child knew the magic of places. And this made my grandfather: places. He wanted to give him a place to [become] man, in an environment where everything conspires so that man forgets his eternal destiny, but now is left without space to think about another life that is immediate and material. And in this search (for his Christian faith, his humanist thought, his poetry in struggle against time) his true relationship with the Twentieth Century was that of a dissident, that of a man against the century in which he was born to live.

The eighth of July, 1999, sick and weak —gravely ill— he was able, with help, to receive his daily communion seated in his bed. At the feet of a Crucified Christ from Colonial times —hung on a wall of his bedroom— there were two consecrated wafers in a silver box. He invoked the Lord and the Lady 'in these decisive hours for me', he gave communion to his grandson and breaking in half the other wafer, shared it with his wife. He prayed a prayer of thanksgiving for the favors he had received in his life, and asked blessings for the two who accompanied him. Here the grandson confronted for the first time the farewell.

The poet survived this crisis of health, but never was the same again. Nor did his body resist for much more time. Somewhat later, rocking in a wheelchair, he told me: 'Aging is death disguised as life.' I stretched to him my hand, while he returned to close his eyes, each time more tired.

The night of Saturday, the 17th of April, 1999, my grandfather went to lie down, but he could not sleep. Towards dawn he was able to get to sleep. And he dreamed of the Virgin Mary. He was in a new island (a small island) making a sculpture. Around him were many like himself, on other little islands, making sculptures of the Lady. Although the next day my grandfather could not reconstruct the dream, he told me that the image was like a review of the many distinct ways of appreciating the qualities (of the Virgin Mary) that he liked the most. But more than that of her physical appearance, he was impacted by her Presence.

Now I know that my grandfather rejoices in the fullness of Heaven. 'Life transforms, it does not end,' says the very ancient preface of the service for the dead. Not of few of us feel grief for his physical absence; but all physical reference is always nothing more in the apparent. From there, I do not have the least doubt, the Poet continues guarding his Country, his 'small Christian country.'

From Chontales to Leon, from North to river, from river to heart.

FOREWORD

by Carlos Mantica
Junio de 2012

There is in a rotunda in Managua a monument with a pedestal several times higher than the statue that sustains it. Without doubt there are many monuments in the world with this characteristic.

The works of men seem to be like the pedestal that elevates to notoriety the hero, the wise one, the poet, the genius, the leader.

But upon the pedestal many times there is a small insignificant man. A weak, corrupt human overcome by vices. A common and ordinary man surprised in a moment of heroism. A complacent doll ready to always say what is great to those who are great and what they want to hear; open to repeat slogans in exchange for applause. To betray friends and betray his own self. Men who give their word, speaking foolishness, accompanying it by saying it well and sounding pretty.

Nicaragua is full of great works produced by very small men. The work of PAC is admirable in its magnitude, profundity, and stature, and should have been more admired if only he had been willing to identify himself with the revolution that betrayed itself. To repeat their slogans. And (he would have been) more honored with prizes internationally if he had only been a little less Christian. But his immense work united, his bronze pedestal could not support the weight nor match the stature of all that is a man called Pablo Antonio Cuadra.

I choose not to write about the work of PAC because others are able to do much better than I, and PAC deserves the best, but I will tell my grandchildren that I knew an extraordinary man who honored me with his friendship.

A JOYFUL BOOK

BOOK OF HOURS

BOOK OF HOURS, WAY OF THE CROSS, AND ROUND OF THE YEAR,

By

PABLO ANTONIO CUADRA

ENGLISH TRANSLATION: SARAH HORNSBY
AND MATTHEW C. HORNSBY

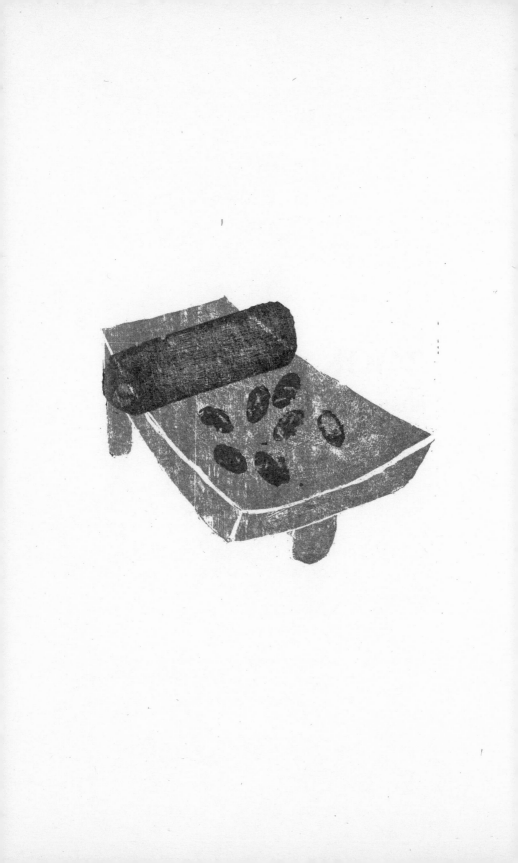

INTRODUCTION

PABLO ANTONIO CUADRA'S BOOK OF HOURS:
BOOK OF HOURS, WAY OF THE CROSS, AND ROUND OF THE YEAR

by Sarah Hornsby

Standing outside looking in the window – that is the position of the foreigner. No matter how long one has lived in the country, no matter how embedded in the life and culture, how many friends, how much reading and studying, there is always more to be learned, absorbed, and understood. After living in Nicaragua for twenty six years, we 'discovered' the Christian writing of Pablo Antonio Cuadra. This translation of his Book of Hours into English is designed to enable you to share in this most exciting adventure.

Pablo Antonio Cuadra, (1912-2002), was Nicaraguan, Christian, journalist, and poet, as well as folklorist, playwright, spanning almost all of that turbulent century with his incredibly insightful prose and poetry. His writing opens a wide and deep view into his world, making *'his vital Nicaraguan experience universal'* in three simultaneous currents: *'a poetry of human solidarity that bears witness to love and faith in Christ as forces of salvation; a poetry of civility and dignity; and a poetry of culture that is a search for the identity, voice and spirit of his people.'*[1]

'He captures the landscape, geography and abundant natural world of Nicaragua and, in the face of foreign intervention, Cuadra exalts a national identity.'[2]

---

1. (White & Arellano, 1988, p.i)
2. (White & Arellano, 1988, p.ii)

Throughout his life, Pablo Antonio Cuadra had the '*moral fiber to confront dictatorships whether leftist or right-wing, to the point that he suffered mistreatment, imprisonments, exiles and persecutions for holding high his indomitable vocation of respect for dialogue and, in this measure, to the integrity, to the projects and the liberty of the 'other'.* '[3]

For the foreigner who comes with this same foundation of respect for dialogue, integrity and liberty, there is welcome. However, there is stern warning for the 'neocolonialists', those who seek to dominate and control Nicaragua, or indeed any of Central and South America, first with 'Manifest Destiny' then with the Monroe Doctrine used by successive U. S. Presidents to justify intervention.[4]

Cuadra says in 'Poem of the Foreigner's Moment in Our Jungle',

I must make something from the mud of history,
dig down in the swamp and unearth the moons of
/my forefathers...
Before my song,
even before I existed,
in the heart of our mountains,
beneath the sordid green of heliconias,
...I invent the stone called flint
and I ignite their white bones delicately polished
/by the ants.[5]

---

3. (Guardia, 2004, 2007, p. 1).
4. The debate over this new spirit of the Monroe Doctrine came to a head in the 1980's, as part of the Iran Contra affair. Among other things, it was revealed that the U.S. Central Intelligence Agency had been covertly training 'Contra' guerrilla soldiers in Honduras in an attempt to destabilize and overthrow the Sandinista revolutionary government of Nicaragua and its' President, Daniel Ortega. CIA director Robert Gates vigorously defended the Contra operation, arguing that avoiding U.S. intervention in Nicaragua would be '*totally to abandon the Monroe doctrine.*' In a case brought before the International Court of Justice by Nicaragua, however, the court ruled that the United States had exercised '*unlawful use of force.*' The U.S. ignored the verdict. (Wikipedia)
5. (White & Arellano, Pablo Antonio Cuadra: The Birth of the Sun: Introduction to the Poetry of Pablo Antonio Cuadra, 1988, p. 15)

The mud of Nicaragua's history included the Filibuster War 1855-1857, in which William Walker from Tennessee and a band of mercenaries, burned Cuadra's hometown of Granada and declared himself President of Nicaragua. Walker hoped to build an empire and powerful slave state three years before the American War between the States.[6][7][8]

In 1909 the dictatorship of Zelaya, who governed the country from 1893, was overthrown by a coalition that included the North American Consul and Pablo Antonio Cuadra's father, Dr. Carlos Cuadra Pasos, orator, lawyer and political conservative. The new Conservative government of Adolfo Diaz repeatedly invited the U.S. Marines to intervene from 1910 to 1933.[9] In July of 1912, the year Cuadra was born; U.S. Marines occupied Nicaragua, requested by the Diaz government. [10]

---

6.   (Cohen, Jonathan: Translator, 1984, 2nd edition 1985, p. 8).
7.   (Kuhl, 2000, p. 439) Walker attempted to sell the Region of Matagalpa for two million dollars to a North American firm. North American investors came for this purpose according to historian Eddy Kuhl.
8.   (Woodward, 2005) In an evaluation of Walker's 1860 account, The War in Nicaragua, Brady Harrison, Professor of English at the University of Montana writes in Agent of Empire: William Walker and the Imperial Self in American Literature that Walker's adventures became a model for the mercenary romance that did much to encourage imperialism. *'Although the mercenary romance may serve as a means to satisfy the reader's desire for action, mystery, and exoticism, it also embodies some of the darkest currents in American culture, notably racism. Latin Americans, these works tell us, cannot govern themselves, cannot rise above bribery and corruption, cannot change leaders without violence, cannot run commercial enterprises, cannot separate church and state. These people —a deplorable mix— of Europeans, Africans, and Indians —must be organized from above.'*
9.   (Lacayo, Un Pobre de Jesus: Padre Azarias H. Pallais, 2000, p. 153)
10. (Lacayo, Un Pobre de Jesus, 2000, pp. 58-63) The conservative government of Albert Diaz overthrew the fifty-four year dictatorship of General Jose Santos Zelaya, who maintained the independence of Nicaragua. In an effort to separate church and state, Zelaya was responsible in 1905 for expelling all Roman Catholic missionaries, the Bishop of Leon, twenty-seven priests and three seminary students. One of those students was

In Cuadra's lifetime, in Central America, the colonial powers of Spain and England were displaced by the new 'imperial power' and the 'yoke' of the Monroe Doctrine of the United States at the beginning of the First World War.

Cuadra's poem about the foreigner's moment in the jungle referred to five hundred North Americans who came to enforce order, burning the huts and killing many of the Indian population in the Segovias, mountainous jungle of northern Nicaragua. They were overcome by malaria and their bones were left in the jungle. This story was made real to the poet who was only fifteen years old when he witnessed the bloody and destructive civil war in 1927; U.S. Marines disembarked in the port of Corinto to support the conservative government of Adolfo Diaz.[11]

As a youth Cuadra formed, with other innovative Catholic Nicaraguan writers, the Vanguard Movement, 1927-1931. In the chaotic aftermath of the First World War, and with Augusto C. Sandino's protest against North American intervention, these writers dared to be different. Rebelling against the Classical/Modernist style of their nation's hero/poet/diplomat, Reuben Dario, they sought to experiment with new forms, new expressions of the vernacular which would represent Nicaraguan identity and its cultural rebirth. Ingenuous, they were hopeful that Somoza's leadership would be a positive force in Nicaragua.[12] Ten years later, however, in 1937, Cuadra was jailed and his magazine censored by Anastasio Somoza Garcia for condoning Sandino's resistance against North American intervention.

Ironically, due to his father's Conservative coalition with Liberal President Somoza, Pablo Antonio Cuadra was designated as a diplomatic representative for Nicaragua. Before the explosion

---

Padre Azarias H. Pallais, then twenty years old, who after being exiled from Nicaragua studied for the priesthood in Paris. He came back to Leon and had enormous, influence on the young Pablo Antonio Cuadra. Their friendship in faith, poetry, compassion for the poor, and dedication to Nicaragua's liberty remained strong until the priest's death in 1954.

11. (Arellano, 1997 second edition, pp. 142-145)
12. (Solis, 2001, pp. 21-22)

of the Second World War, Cuadra travelled widely in Central and South America, Mexico, Spain, Italy, France and North Africa. His early writings were published in Chile, Spain, and Brazil. Some of his first books of essays anticipated the Book of Hours.[13]

Cuadra had become well known for his studies of Nicaraguan culture, music, folklore and archeological research which were represented in his poetry, journalism and creative theatrical productions. He delighted in writing about the occupations and everyday concerns of the people of Nicaragua. He used the common terms he heard from ordinary farmers, foresters, fishermen, seamen, citing the seasons and stars of the Southern Cross. This familiar Nicaraguan vocabulary was augmented by his use of extensive literary, geographical and Biblical comparisons, such as comparing his Great Lake with Galilee, or its seamen with Ulysses and his Odyssey. Much of his writing focused on the fusion of Indian and Spanish, mestizo roots shared with so many Nicaraguans – proud, intelligent, astute, nationalistic, defiant, resistant to foreign intrusion, especially North American, yet absorbing and using to best advantage whatever that foreigner brings to the mix.

In 1944 Cuadra was inducted into the prestigious Academia Nicaragüense de la Lengua, correspondant to the Royal Spanish Academy by his mentor, poet and priest, Padre Azarias H. Pallais, chaplain of the Vanguard and respected member of the Academy. (*see footnote 11*)

'PAC,' as Cuadra was known, left Nicaragua with his family and some of his Vanguard group in disfavor with the Somoza dynasty, to live in self-exile in Mexico from 1945-1948. There he began writing the Book of Hours. *This work fuses the spirit and form of the medieval books of hours, and the poetry and songs from pre-Colombian Indian codices binding time and nature to the Christian mysteries.*[14] '*In the midst of this uncertainty – interior and*

---

13. (White, El Mundo Mas Que Humano en la Poesia de Pablo Antonio Cuadra: Un Estudio Ecocritico, 2002, p. 66)
14. (Solis, Prologo a Poesia I, 2003, p. x)

global – he had two transforming experiences: that of the Indian in his religiosity and his sense of time (impacted...by the conversion of the Indian Juan Diego); and the magic touch of the indigenous past.[15]

This fusion of the historical and mythical in his writing can be compared to the works of C.S. Lewis, who brought the English Arthurian legends to life in his Space Trilogy and Narnian Chronicles. Lewis used the myths to undergird and enhance the communication of his deeply Christian world view, and PAC does the same from a Central American context.

Upon the failure of his journal, Editorial Suma, in 1948, PAC accepted a position in Santander, Spain to teach Spanish American literature, where he became corresponding member of the Royal Spanish Academy. Returning to Nicaragua from Europe, disillusioned with the abuses of power of Franco and Mussolini, he became Director of La Prensa in 1953. It was during these stressful years, 1946-1954, that PAC continued writing the Book of Hours. PAC, with Pedro Joaquin Chamorro, journalist-owner of La Prensa, wrote courageously, and were jailed and tortured with hundreds of other suspected enemies by Luis Somoza after his father, Anastasio Somoza Garcia's assassination in 1956.

Again in the 1980's he was also censured and went into exile due to the pressures of the Sandinista government. Cuadra wrote poetry and prose prolifically throughout all those turbulent times. He was recognized and honored by foreigners, while those in power in his own country viewed his creative ideas with fear and paranoia.

Open, honest, analytical, Pablo Antonio Cuadra pierced, penetrated and published his views on the dualities of being Nicaraguan. In the introduction to his best seller, El Nicaragüense, PAC writes:

Poetry, the creative work – including certain letters – is not conceived except by the hand, its ink flowing like

---

15. (Solis Cuadra, Pablo Antonio Cuadra: Itinerario, 2008, pp. 51-52)

blood. Because of this there is one part of me, from brain to heart, from heart to hand, that jealously goes apart, labors in silence, solitary, painfully slow, with my own handwriting.

The work of the journalist, on the other hand, that of editor, traveler, critic, the one who writes neatly because of deadline pressures and the press, between noises, interruptions, visits, dialogues, unexpected impressions, readings without sediment, and telephones... goes from the mind to the keyboard, is conceived with velocity, in a hasty heart and written by machine.[16]

PAC's writings are deeply Christian, exemplarily Roman Catholic. His Way of the Cross, Via Crucis, is a meditation on the fourteen Stations of the Cross, which traditionally, many, before and since, have interpreted in paintings, relief sculptures, poetry and prose. Cuadra's poetic rendering of those fourteen themes for meditation are of such high caliber that they were chosen by Pope John Paul II to use in Rome in 1986.

It is through the window of Cuadra's Christian writings that I chose to focus, because the mutual framework of faith was my husband Jim's and my reason for coming to Nicaragua. We came to Nicaragua to make an incarnational statement, as North American followers of the living Jesus, against the covert war of aggression in the 1980's. Then we stayed on to retire in Nicaragua, because we had found a place and a work here that God began with us, which continued through five successive governments.

Even within the framework of Biblical faith, Cuadra's view was Roman Catholic and mine was Presbyterian Protestant, of which there were no churches when we first came to Nicaragua in 1984. To demonstrate how small a view I had from my window, we lived in three areas of Nicaragua for twenty-three years before I 'discovered' the writings of Pablo Antonio Cuadra, published in

16. (Cuadra, El Nicaragüense, 1993; 13th edition 2004, p. 11)

several volumes as a 'Cultural Collection of Central America' by the Accessorial Consultant Group and Uno Bank of Nicaragua. These were edited by his grandson, Pedro Xavier Solis, as part of their service of rescuing the cultural heritage of the people of Nicaragua. The bank sent us Poesia I as a Christmas gift, and so the adventure began.

Reading and re-reading Cuadra's Book of Hours, with dictionary in hand, brought new images and understandings to mind, heart and spirit. My perceptions were deepened and enlivened and my own faith inspired, as well as raising many questions. Still I persisted, realizing my Spanish was not good enough to comprehend everything. Cuadra used many terms from his intimate knowledge of Nicaraguan culture, customs, languages, including Nahuatl, as well as classical and street, city and country Spanish. Like a *native Adam, the poet names the things of the world around him – innumerable quantities of natural and human elements that belong to an agricultural tradition with colonial roots.*[17] PAC delighted in naming the tropical flora and fauna, fish and birds that he knew in his native colonial city of Granada near Nicaragua's Great Lake and in the grasslands of Chontales that he traveled on horseback.

My window in Nicaragua, besides PAC's writing, has been opened thanks to the gracious invitation of Don Francisco Arellano of PAVSA publishing house. Arellano, Director of the Academia Nicaragüense de la Lengua, knew PAC well and introduced me to Steven White, Lawrence University professor. As a college student White knew PAC during a summer working at La Prensa in Managua, and continued his friendship. White shared many experiences with PAC, analyzing and translating several books of his poetry, especially focusing on his 'eco-poetry', poetry that has ecological implications. Pedro Xavier Solís contributed with permissions, and his book, Pablo Antonio Cuadra – Itinerary, gave needed historical perspective and orientation.

---

17. (White & Arellano, Pablo Antonio Cuadra: The Birth of the Sun: Introduction to the Poetry of Pablo Antonio Cuadra, 1988, p. iii)

Getting to know PAC has opened to me other amazing windows – his mentors and literary friends, like Padre Azarías H. Pallais. Poet and priest, Padre Azarías was chaplain of the young Vanguard group of writers. He is considered one of the three greatest Nicaraguan poets after Rubén Darío, and was very influential in many aspects of PAC's faith and life.

Reading PAC introduced me not only to other Nicaraguan poets and writers, but to the innumerable '*Tribe*'[18] of European and other writers who he knew in person or avidly read, studied, and included in his intellectual and spiritual development. PAC was director of La Prensa newspaper from 1953-1998, where he shared with his friend, Pedro Joaquin Chamorro, the pressures and dangers of speaking out with courage in the face of imprisonment and exile. Pedro Joaquin was assassinated by the Somoza regime in 1978, and his martyrdom led to the overthrow of that government. His widow, Violetta Chamorro, became the first elected president of Nicaragua after the revolution.

Ernesto Cardenal, PAC's nephew, is another key figure, who has given insight into his life and times. Ernesto had been with PAC in exile in Mexico. He then spent two years, from 1957-1959, in the Cistercian order in Gethsemane, Kentucky, under the tutelage of Thomas Merton. Both Cardenal and PAC maintained a lively literary correspondence with Thomas Merton, much of which is published.[19]

Merton wrote Cuadra in 1958 while translating The Jaguar and the Moon: *I spent some very pleasant afternoons under the silent trees translating your poems – a work, like all monastic work, consecrated, something that the profound seriousness of the poem deserves. I am overjoyed at their originality and spiritual independence in taking and using the Indian religious tradition as our Christian property. We have an enormous debt to repay to the*

---

18. (Cuadra, Poesia II, 2003, p. 260)
19. (Bochen, 1993, pp. xiii; 78-79; 113; 117; 124; 126-127; 134-138; 141-142; 147-148; 156; 158; 160)

Indians, and we should at least begin by recognizing the spiritual richness of the Indian religious genius. '[20]

In 1962 Merton wrote Pablo Antonio Cuadra a letter which was a stunning vision of the perilous situation of the world at the mercy of two nuclear giants, Russia and the United States.[21]

'*The shocking thing is that the whole world is being pulled this way and that by two enormous powers that are both practically insane and both insane in the same way, with the same paranoid obsession with power, the same fascination with technological expansion, the same vulgarity, the same brutal stupidity and insensitivity to human and spiritual values (although in the U.S. religion is cynically supposed to be blessing the whole system), the same callous addiction to super-myths and the same helpless immersion in materialism.*[22]

PAC wrote in '*The Tribe*,' about Ernesto and their friend, Trappist monk, Thomas Merton:

> *The Trappist (vow) is silence, but they allowed him to speak with me:*
> *'The Beauty that the poet produces is part of the Kingdom,' he told me.*
> *Later he warned me, in a letter, against the Giants against Gog*
> *and Magog*
> *(because the American man has not overcome the stage of the Giants).*
> *And we spoke under the moon of the founding of Solentiname.*
> *But now [he did not live] to see Ernesto of beret and machine-gun*
> *Convert his Benedictine dream into a school where it was taught to kill with love...* '[23]

---

20. (Bochen, 1993, p. 180)
21. (Bochen, 1993, p. 126)
22. (Cuadra, Ensayos II;, 2003, pp. 236-252)
23. (Cuadra, Poesia II, 2003, pp. 268-269)

Merton died in 1968; Ernesto Cardenal began his Community of Faith in Solentiname, on the archipelago of Nicaragua's Great Lake, Cocibolca, early in the 1970's. The Somoza dictatorship destroyed Solentiname, and the painful struggle is vividly described in Cardenal's autobiographical <u>La Revolución Perdida</u>.[24] The revolution triumphed in 1979, the same year Ronald Reagan defeated Jimmy Carter as President of the United States. Ernesto Cardenal, Catholic priest/poet and Minister of Culture for the Sandinista government, was censured by the same pope who commended PAC in 1986 for his Via Crucis that is included here.

My youngest son, Matt, came with us to Nicaragua in the eighties when he was eight years old, lived with us in those first early years in rural Chinandega, in the capital city of Managua, and the northern mountains of Matagalpa. Matt continued his education and work in the U.S. until he returned to Matagalpa and married Nohelia Talavera in 2008. Nohelia's extensive family has included us in their celebrations and given us another window through which to see and understand Nicaraguan life.

My Nicaraguan prayer group, led by our friend, Doña Julia Cardoza, is my most consistent window into Nicaraguan life. In that group I am different, always, but also included as one of them. When they say, '*Sarita is one of us, Nicaragüense*,' that is the highest compliment that can be given, for it is the gift of acceptance and belonging. In Christ Jesus those barriers no longer are impenetrable, but open a way where there is no way.

In Pablo Antonio Cuadra's writing I recognized that same Holy Spirit that was poured out on believers, of many languages and countries, at Pentecost, who, in a fresh outpouring, touched and transformed many in Catholic and Protestant Churches worldwide in the 1960's. One of the first people Jim and I met in Nicaragua was Carlos Mantica, who spearheaded the Cursillo Movement in Nicaragua and led the Catholic Charismatic Renewal Movement. Carlos was close friend of PAC's in faith, in deep love of discovering their Nahuatl roots and culture in song, stories, and language. Like

---

24. (Cardenal, 2004 2nd Edition)

PAC, Carlos Mantica is a member of the Academia Nicaragüense de la Lengua, and enabled this translation to be published. There is an unforgettable vignette about PAC in one of Carlos' books which I append to PAC's <u>Book of Hours</u>, since it gives such a colorful picture of the two men.[25]

In an email answering some of my pesky questions, Carlos responded: *'Pablo was an exemplary Christian and his faith very solid and unbreakable.'*

My prayer for you, dear reader, is that this translation may serve as a window for you to discover some of the deep wisdom from the Christian faith and Nicaraguan experience of Pablo Antonio Cuadra.

October 2012,
Matagalpa, Nicaragua

———————————————

25. (Mantica A., 2007, pp. 104-106)   Carlos Mantica wrote to the editor the following in an email: *I had the privilege to be a very good friend of PAC during various decades. Though he was not an active leader in the Charismatic Renewal, but he was an active leader in Christian Cursillos. He participated in the 8th Curcillo in Managua in 1968, and immediately joined with much joy my weekly 'Group Meeting'; he accompanied me as Leader in the 10th Cursillo in 1972 giving it what we call the Lay Role, on the occasion of the Second Central American Ultreya, attended by several thousand people from all of Central America. I was a stupendous talk that we printed and that I hope to find in my disorderly archives.*

PREFACE

To Pablo Antonio Cuadra's
BOOK OF HOURS: Breviary of the course of time of the heart and hope of a Christian poet: 1945-1954

by Sarah Hornsby

Pablo Antonio Cuadra was writing his Book of Hours between 1946-1954 during which time he was in self-exile in Mexico and Spain for three years, then back in Nicaragua. Impelled by conflicts with the Somoza dynasty, and profoundly impacted by the civil war in Spain and the Second World War, PAC came to a re-discovery of hope in Christ as the '*point where time and eternity cross.*'[1]

White emphasizes that Cuadra's first four published books of prose,[2] before beginning the Book of Hours, developed his thought that Medieval Christianity, i.e. Catholicism, was the ideal to be fervently pursued. He considered it 'a new crusade' against the hammer and sickle of communism, which he likened to the medieval crusades against the Moslems. A fundamental idea in his poetry is that the union of Medieval Europe with the Americas reflects the experience of Colonialization. White notes that PAC's earlier book, Imperial Breviary, for example, is a manifestation of great political-religious fervor, with Cuadra proposing a kind of holy war. '*We are and we have to be crusaders to truly respond to the immense inheritance that our founders have left us.*'[3]

---

1. (Yepes Boscan, 1996, p. ii)
2. Toward the Cross of the South (1938), Imperial Breviary (1940), Promotion from Mexico and other essays (1945) and Between the Cross and the Sword (map of essays for the rediscovery of America (1946)
3. (White, El Mundo Mas Que Humano en la Poesia de Pablo Antonio Cuadra: Un Estudio Ecocritico, 2002, pp. 66-67)

Later Cuadra would speak of those early years as having '*a dangerous politization of his religious faith.*' Concerning Ernesto Cardenal's involvement in the armed resistance of the Revolution, Cuadra said, '*to politicize religion produces immediately, fanaticism...I committed this error/sin as a youth. For that reason I do not want to commit it in my old age.*' So White proposes that Cuadra rejected the Middle Ages for the modern age in political terms, but guarded the religious faith associated with that period. His Book of Hours was an expression of his faith, a 'New-Medieval' way of reconstruction by means of prayer.[4]

Cuadra chose the Medieval Book of Hours as a structure, a 'dwelling for his religious poetry. Traditionally the Gothic Cathedral was the culmination of the highest artistic achievement of Medieval Civilization, and a Book of Hours was designed to be a book of prayers, a cathedral that can be held in ones hands. At a time when only the very wealthy or nobility could have the Bible, the increasing popularity and availability of Books of Hours linked church and home. These books, in both Roman and Anglican traditions, included a Perpetual Calendar, the life of Christ from the Gospels, prayers for meditation on the 'Hours' of the Virgin Mary, the Passion cycle, the Hours of the Cross, and the Hours of the Holy Spirit. Penitential Psalms[5] were included, Memorials or suffrages[6], naming saints, their lives, and special intercessions.[7]

The entrance into this holy space was the Holy Virgin Mary. She was honored as being the one through whom God entered

---

4.   Ibid. p. 77
5.   The **Penitential Psalms or Psalms of Confession**, so named in Casiodo-rus's commentary of the 6th century AD, are the Psalms 6, 32, 38, 51, 102, 130 and 143 (6, 31, 37, 50, 101, 129, and 142 in the Septuagint numbering). These are especially expressive of sorrow for sin. Four were known as 'penitential psalms' by St. Augustine of Hippo in the early 5th century. The fifty-first Psalm (*Miserere*) was recited at the close of daily morning service in the primitive Church. (Wikipedia)
6.   Suffrages - a listing of Saints, both universally recognized and obscure. The reader calls upon each saint and offers a prayer, in hopes of being forgiven for previous sins. (Patrick Kempe web page.)
7.   (Wieck, 1988)

humanity, birthing the Son, who made possible new birth and everlasting life for every believer. Cuadra, by referring to this design creates a 'parenthesis', beginning his Book of Hours with the '*Hymn of Hours to the Eyes of Our Lady*' and concluding with the Round of the Year with '*December: Our Lady of the Blue Shawl*' and '*Final Song to Our Lady*.'[8]

Entering the Book of Hours, the poet describes Mary in three poems in one '*Hymn of Hours to the Eyes of Our Lady*.' Three aspects are seen: first Mary, the Daughter of God in the Annunciation through blue eyes of Faith; second is Mary, the Mother of God the Son in the Nativity/ Christmas through green eyes of Hope; third is Mary, the Bride of the Holy Spirit, Wife of God in the Passion of Christ, seen through black eyes of Charity or suffering Love.

Blue describes Faith – the heavenlies, creation of water/air, and the creatures that swim and fly in them, birds/fish. From the beginning of time God had in mind Mary's overcoming faith at the Angel's Annunciation. The poet asks to see through her eyes, through our tears, to see those first waters of creation, contemplate the Annunciation of who Jesus was and is, the Fish, acrostic in Greek for Jesus Christ, Son of God, Savior. He asks that we may have this overcoming faith.

Green describes Hope – the Nativity, the Birth of Jesus at Christmas, Fecund Mother Earth is described by naming Biblical trees and places, the fragrances, and fertility of earth's greenness. Here the poet relates Time to the changing Seasons and the music of forest and wind that carries the '*tenuous cry of the children.*' Mary blesses the '*flourishing wombs' that 'cross the poplar groves of your eyes.*'

PAC experienced, while in exile in Mexico, the places where the Virgin of Guadalupe appeared to the peasant, Juan Diego in the 15th century. His '*tilma*', a rustic one piece garment, was miraculously imprinted with the image of a brown-skinned Mary which hangs in the Basilica in Mexico City. Studies have been made of the eyes of Mary in this painting, and miniature families

8.   Ibid. pp. 61-63.

can be seen in the pupils of her eyes. Perhaps it was this that is echoed in these poems to the eyes of Our Lady.

Mary, the Light filled Mother, Jesus being the Light that comes into the world through her, reveals the *'germinating song of the mornings,'* leading to *'the congregation of the wheat fields.'* Jesus said a grain of wheat must die so that laborers can harvest the ripe fields. Mary sees also the grape being prepared, the new wine. Jesus described at the Last Supper his body as the bread of life and his blood as the wine poured out, and that we are to taste and see that he is good. Here the poet's symbol is the Lamb, the perfect Lamb of God, who is the sacrifice born of Mary in a stable, worshipped by poverty shepherds at Christmas.

Playfully the poet remembers his own infancy at Christmas, and the Nicaraguan customs he recalls. He seems to refer to the Nativity Scenes of Bethlehem, the Crèche displayed each year in many churches, using *'moss from the mountains.'* These nativities enabled the young PAC to see those miniature fields through Mary's eyes. He pictures the *'little Indians entering on their knees,'* and that has been a custom in Nicaragua, as it still is in Mexico and other Catholic Latin American countries. Playfully PAC imagines Mary singing lullabies both to baby Jesus and to all the children. There is, however, poignancy in these songs, because Mary's eyes are wet as with dew thinking of future pain prophesied.

Still Christmas is a time of Hope. PAC says that to return to that moment is to return, from all the noise and distractions of the world and the *'useless windows'* to hope. *'Open your eyes, oh Mother of memories.'* The poet wants Mary to look at him with Bethlehem, because he desires the innocence of his childhood.

The third poem of the Hours of the Mary Trilogy is <u>Black which describes Charity or Love</u>. Black are the eyes of Mary in the Passion; she experienced all the grief and pain of Jesus on the Cross as burning, scorched, solitary eyes flooded with tears, left in ashes. All the pain of History, from the errors of the first Eve and her son, Abel, pass through Mary's eyes. The poet wonders if Mary, *'wounded white lily'* still trembles with those moans of grief for the suffering of mankind.

This Mary of the black eyes identifies with the suffering of everyone who has experienced horrible loss of a loved one. She is *'Lady of death', 'Mother of affliction, Crucified heart', 'painful Eve.'* Other symbols expressed are that Mary is the new Eve, and the Cross is the new Tree of Paradise. In her eyes can be seen the shadow where *'love resides...joined to the Cross that is lifted in her eyes.'*[9]

As the new or second Eve, Mary's exemplary life inspires the poet to offer his own life – to eat the *'burning apple', giver of new life that lays down its own life.'* Mary was told in Luke's Gospel, Chapter 1, by the prophet, Simeon, that a sword would pierce her heart as it would her Son's. So with Mary's pierced heart the poet seeks to identify and give his life.

In Hebrews 4:12-13, reference is made to the Sword that the Spirit wields, which is the double-edged sword of the Word of God that pierces *'as far as the division of soul and spirit, of both joints and marrow, and able to judge the thoughts and intentions of the heart...all things are open and laid bare to the eyes of Him with whom we have to do.'*[10] Could it be that the poet alludes to that sword of the Word of God that cleanses as it cuts, the living Word of God which is Jesus?

According to Yepes Boscan in his Introduction to the Book of Hours, PAC utilized the ancient monastic system of dividing the day into times of prayer: Dawn, Morning, Evening and Night. *'Each moment of prayer in this Book of Hours is headed by a 'Chapter' associated with one of the four elements: water, air, fire and earth, integrated by a variable number of poems that enclose symbols, mysteries expressing the grief, joy and hopes of the Christian. In this collection of poems Cuadra verbalizes 'saving grace, the gifts and closeness of the Holy Spirit, and the insinuating Presence of God.'*[11]

---

9.   (Solis, Prologo a Poesia I, 2003, p. 324)
10.   (The New Open Bible Study Edition, 1990)
11.   (Yepes Boscan, 1996, pp. iv-v)

Dawn awakens the sleeper from his dreams. He awakens to new opportunities, to new appreciation of the everyday labors for the Homeland (Patria). The poet appreciates nature's beauty, bounty, and wonders. Hope arrives each dawn with everything being new with promise, with anything being possible. There also seems to be an allusion to the more distant future promised in Isaiah 65:17 and in Revelation 21:1, the 'recreation' of a new heaven and a new earth.

In 'Choral to the poets of the dawn' and in 'National Hymn', dawn is associated with Water, and celebrates the creation of the landscape, specifically the nation and the 'new-men,' who have drunk the 'wine of the morning' and the 'juice of the dawn.' Cuadra names birds found in Nicaragua as well as the common names of his Nicaraguan countrymen and their everyday labors and songs, thus in his Book of Hours time is viewed very specifically from Nicaraguan perspective.

> To you, Jose Muñoz, carpenter by trade, who knows how to make my table, take this star. It comes out to guide your hour. Put it together!
>
> And you, Martin Zepeda, well, you go walking, rustle these birds. Give them song or tell them what you know of bread and the guitar.
>
> And to you, Pedro Canisal, cowboy, rustic youth: saddle the horizon, ride to the end of the night, tame it!
>
> Everyone dream. Everyone show that you are with me making this future day, svelte and without anguish. [12]

Morning prayer, identified with Air, is the invocation of the Holy Spirit to come into the everyday sustenance of laborers, into the wheat and the growers of wheat: 'Elemental time of bread and of wine. Of wheat and of the new word.' [13] Cuadra infers that the Eucharist is the very sustenance of life, quenching hunger and blessing with life the labors of every person.

---

12. (Solis, Prologo a Poesia I, 2003, p. 330)
13. Ibid. p. 334

Steven White asserts that in these early poems of Dawn and Morning PAC, especially *'Chorale of the Poets of the Dawn'*, also reflected his studies of Garibay in Mexico. Garibay describes the common Nahuatl word form as *'flowering word'*, *'cuicatl,'* or as music with or without words adorned with flowers.[14] The category of poetry which White sees in PAC's Dawn and Morning poems is *'Xochicuicatl'*, song of flowers, poems in Nahuatl that are hymns of praise, to be sung directly to the gods. The more anguished poems of Afternoon and Night contain the form of *'Icnocuicatl'*, which were Nahuatl songs of desolation and feeling orphaned.[15] which is a perfect 'counter-discourse' to the purpose of the Book of Hours.

'Invitation to the Vagabonds' is a poignant poem bringing into focus the depths of longing evoked by the Nicaraguan experience of exile. It is made even more expressive since it was the reality from which PAC was writing. Many Scriptural images are brought to mind through his descriptions of the agony of the exile's separation from all that he loves about his country.

'We see the poet with his inadmissible suit of melancholy,' seems to evoke the Banquet in the Kingdom of God, where the person is refused admission for not wearing the garment of praise, joy, thanksgiving and gratitude given by the host.

PAC concludes with the revelation of the *'ultimate beggar'* who comes to the table, lays aside his worn walking stick, opens his travel bag and takes the bread and upon breaking it, *'our eyes are opened.'* This is what happened to the two disciples on the Emmaus Road after Jesus' resurrection, but PAC brings it into the context of recognizing Jesus in the midst of Nicaraguan poverty. The Risen Jesus is revealed in the midst of the Nicaraguan experience of physical hunger and of seeking to know God.[16] Here the images come to mind of PAC wandering the countryside with his mentor and friend, Padre Azarias H. Pallais, who had a special love for the

14. (Alcina Franch, 189-2008, pp. 19-21)
15. (White, El Mundo Mas Que Humano en la Poesia de Pablo Antonio Cuadra: Un Estudio Ecocritico, 2002, pp. 86-87) (Ed. More on White's analysis of Garibay in the 'Night' section of Book of Hours)
16. (Solis, Prologo a Poesia I, 2003, pp. 336-339)

poor and, with a Francis of Assisi spirit, shared generously of his sustenance, both physical and spiritual.[17]

'*Prayer in the Forest*' is an eco-poem (1993) invoking the preservation of the wealth of botanical diversity in a Great Chain of Being that PAC wanted included in his final publication of the Book of Hours.[18] White quotes Kirkpatrick Sale as saying that the Medieval Franciscan ideal of seeing Christ in every creature has been viewed as limited, since the a-biotic elements of light, temperature, atmosphere, water, chemicals, were ignored. However in PAC's Book of Hours, these very elements are present and received with gratitude.

Cuadra emphasizes that in the '*Hymn to the Son,*' Saint Francis calls water, earth, fruits and flowers his brothers. '*This is not lyricism in the superficial sense, but poetry in its essential meaning of the act of creation.*'[19] Here is where White describes the beautiful and fundamental relationship that PAC discovered in his studies of Garibay in Mexico, and which he subtly included in his poetry/ prayers, the affinity between the ideal new medieval Christian society and the great diversity of Pre-Colombian indigenous cultures and literature.[20]

---

17. (Arguello Lacayo, 2000, p. 121) 'Pablo Antonio Cuadra has preserved for us a marvelous image of Pallais during these walks to the country-side, that merit being translated to painting: 'Among many unforgettable memories of his friendship, I remember a hike with Padre Azarias, cross-ing mountains and trails and leagues and leagues – we crossed a plain inundated, with the water up to the waist and he, with his torn cassock in loud voice reciting Alejandrino verses or citing Hesiod in Greek – and I saw him visit the farms of the country folk and talk with them of the Good News in his familiar style that was always poetry in the colloquial. I remember him, now in the afternoon, soaked by the rain, sitting on a stool, drinking from a '*Jicaro*' gourd of tepid '*pinol* ' smoky under the palm thatched roof and speaking to them in the same way that he wrote his parables or 'evangelized words' while at the same time outside the birds passed under the insistent rough wet winds.'

18. (White, El Mundo Mas Que Humano en la Poesia de Pablo Antonio Cuadra: Un Estudio Ecocritico, 2002, pp. 79-80)

19. Ibid. p. 80

20. (Garibay K., 1992, p. 103)

Mexican Roman Catholic priest, Angel Maria Garibay K., philologist, linguist, historian, scholar of pre-Colombian (1892-1967), was publishing his studies and translations of Nahuatl poetry, and History of the Literature Nahautl, while PAC, in exile, was also in Mexico writing the greater part of his poems for his Book of Hours (1945-1948).[21] White suggests putting the text of the Nahautl poems used by Garibay side by side with PAC's 'counter-discourse' of the great diversity of pre-Colombian indigenous cultures to understand how much those ancient writings affected the poet in broadening his vision to include those symbols and mysteries as well. '... *the presence of a phrase in the Nahuatl language in the poetry of Cuadra is simply an invitation to blend in a deeper symbolic level.'*[22] The '*flowering butterfly*' was symbol in Nahuatl of the poet, whose purpose is to express praise to the gods, and painted as if the words coming forth from the poet were lovely flowers.[23]

Yepes Boscan, the theologian who wrote the official Introduction to the 1997 edition of the Venezuelan Book of Hours approved by PAC, is critiqued by White for not taking note of this 'counter-discourse.' White implies that Boscan either did not see or did not agree with this element of combining '*excessive*' Catholic theology with the writings of Nahuatl origins. Whereas Garibay notes that from much of the Aztec writings, Christians who gathered these poems tried to '*eliminate names of gods, or substitute them for names of beings that Christianity venerates.*' Cuadra dares to reclaim the indigenous gods that were erased by the (Spanish) Conquest, and in some of his later poems dramatically converses with them, a technique used by Ignatius of Loyola to make Bible

---

21. Other Nicaraguan writers from the Vanguard group – Ernesto Cardenal and Ernesto Mejia Sanchez were studying in the National Autonomous University of Mexico. (from Introduction to bilingual edition by Russell O. Salmon, 1991, of Golden UFO's: the Indian Poems, by Ernesto Cardenal (ed.)
22. (White, El Mundo Mas Que Humano en la Poesia de Pablo Antonio Cuadra: Un Estudio Ecocritico, 2002, p.81)
23. (Alcina Franch, 189-2008, p. 21)

reading come alive, which PAC probably learned early from his Jesuit teachers.'[24] [25]

PAC, himself, wrestled with the inner conflict caused by being 'mestizo', having both Indian and Spanish heritage, and wrote much about his struggle to accept this dual history/ heritage in both his poetry and prose.[26]

Afternoon for PAC begins with the completely Scriptural description of the crucifixion which was at midday, the sixth hour, '*And it was now about the sixth hour, and darkness fell over the whole land until the ninth hour.* ' (Luke 24:44). The 'Sext' hour, noon, was one of the canonical hours, or offices of prayer.

In the introductory 'Chapter' of Afternoon, Jesus is identified as the Word: '*In the beginning was the Word, and the Word was with God, and the Word was God...And the Word became flesh, and dwelt among us, and we beheld His glory...*' (John 1:14) Jesus had said, '*I am the good shepherd, and I know My own and My own know Me.*' (John 10:14) '*Christ also is the head of the church. He Himself being the Savior of the Body.*' (Ephesians 5:23) And John's Revelation is affirmed: '*And I saw heaven opened; and behold, a white horse, and He who sat upon it is called Faithful and True; and in righteousness He judges and wages war. And His eyes are a flame of fire...He is clothed with a robe dipped in blood; and His name is called 'The Word of God...King of Kings and Lord of Lords...*' (Revelation 19:11-16)[27]

Afternoon, identified with fire, is '*associated with the elements of the Passion of Christ: tree, wood, iron, leather, thorny bramble bush, saliva, all of which were the material from which were made the instruments of the Passion: cross, whip, nails, crown of thorns, lance, ridicules, humiliations, and bitterness.*'[28]

---

24. (White, El Mundo Mas Que Humano en la Poesia de Pablo Antonio Cuadra: Un Estudio Ecocritico, 2002, p. 83)
25. (Solis, Prologo a Poesia I, 2003, pp.185-311) El Jaguar y la Luna (poesía indígena); El Nican-Nauat; El Indio y el Violin.
26. Especially in *Round of the Year*, the last section of the Book of Hours. Note in the Appendix the Essay: Christian Formation of America (ed.)
27. (The New Open Bible Study Edition, 1990)
28. (Yepes Boscan, 1996, p. v)

'...unless a grain of wheat falls into the earth and dies, it remains by itself alone; but if it dies, it bears much fruit.' (John 12:24)

Using the vivid Scarlet Letter, 'A' for adulterer image, the poet uses the tree image for Jesus on the cross, the 'Alpha and Omega', the first and last letter of the Greek alphabet, the beginning and the end, nailed to the tree. (Revelation 22:13) The image of a letter written in blood is of the Tau cross, the letter God instructed the Children of Israel in Egypt to write with the blood of the Passover Lamb on the doorposts of their houses, so that the death angel would pass over. Jesus is that Passover Lamb. *'And the blood will be a sign for you on the houses where you live; and when I see the blood I will pass over you, and no plague will befall you to destroy you when I strike the land of Egypt.'* (Exodus 12:1-14)[29]

'Testament' is a possible reference to both the Old Testament and the New Testament in the Bible. First appears the Tree of Knowledge in Genesis guarded by an angel in Paradise. At the end of the Bible, in Revelation, appears the Tree of Life, whose leaves are for the healing of the nations.[30]

Ark and rainbow: refers to Noah's ark made of wood, and *'arco-iris'*, in Spanish, is the rainbow, symbol of God's promise of protection. (Genesis 9) 'Iris' is also the colored part of the eye, another reference by PAC to 'eyes' from the three poems to Our Lady at the beginning of the Book of Hours.

In a rare reference to Protestants as well as Roman Catholics, PAC pictures the Church as a ship carrying *'uncomfortable and brothers, protesters of the wind or wise opposers of the route;'* sing *the navigating Church'* [31] The *Fisherman* – Peter, disciple, apostle of Jesus, was a fisherman who Jesus said would be head of the Church, to make fishers of men. (Matthew 16:18, Matthew 4:19)[32]

---

29. (The New Open Bible Study Edition, 1990)
30. Tree of Knowledge of Good and Evil in Genesis 2:15-17; 3:24; Tree in Paradise in Revelation's New Jerusalem – Revelation 22:1-2. (ed.)
31. (Cuadra, Poesia I, 2003, p. 343)
32. (The New Open Bible Study Edition, 1990)

Jesus looking over Jerusalem wept before entering the city wept: '*O Jerusalem, Jerusalem, the city that kills the prophets and stones those sent to her! How often I wanted to gather your children together, just as a hen gathers her brood under her wings, and you would not have it!*' (Luke 13:34) From this quotation PAC derives the imagery of a '*Feathered Cross*', an early allusion to the Quetzalcoatl, to be described later.

In the cross that ends the life of the Word of God, the poet sees reflected every creature and the cross is remembered in every vertex and crossroads:

> *When the Man said his last word,*
> *darkness and shadows were lifted.*
> *All creatures were in the chalice of darkness,*
> *All creatures were of the lineage of shadows.*
> *'Listen!' – they said – We have been constructed in the*
> *likeness of this tree,*
> *and every creature's flower was marked by his sign!*
> *The vertex[33] of the winds sings his sign,*
> *the union of the elements, and the cross-roads!*
> *Every bird that spreads its wings to sustain the song*
> *of its route*
> *Every gathering of stars over the four points of*
> *destiny*
> *Every man extended for love*
> *commemorates the impassible balance of your*
> *judgment:*
> *Oh, blessed support! Oh, fertile equilibrium! Oh,*
> *faithful Cross!'[34]*

'*Christ in the Afternoon*' evokes both the culmination of that torture and death on the cross and Jesus, alive, walking again those dusty roads with the ordinary companions, doing the everyday things that become so meaningful since he has overcome death!

---

33. In geometry, a vertex (plural vertices) is a special kind of point that describes the corners or intersections of geometric shapes. (Wikipedia)
34. (Solis, Prologo a <u>Poesia I</u>, 2003, p. 345)

In the same way, Boscan assures, *'night or the Apocalypse, is poetic symbol of the contradictory condition of man and of his broken, torn essentials. Lyrical expression of the opposites that nest in the heart of the human being: infinite supernatural joys and inexpressible earthly frights...wedding nights and nights of agonies, fusion and fixed boundaries, of suffering and joys, of faith and doubt, the serpent and the Quetzal, of sin and grace...* [35]

> *Serpent that slithers in its exile, seeking completion in the Quetzal of auroral plumes. Night like the cry in this valley of tears. Night in the sinistral of the dream.*
>
> *Left of death. Silence of the great struggle, night of weddings and of agonies. Of infinite joys and inexplicable frights.*
>
> *Night of Eve, of Peter, of Judas, of the sinner. Night of the coming of the Bridegroom* [36]*: 'media nocte clamor jactus est..'*
>
> *Night or the Apocalypse.* [37]

Here is the first direct reference to Quetzalcoatl, the Toltec, Aztec, Nahuatl god-figure, the dualistic serpent/Quetzal, exotic Tropical bird that is national bird of Guatemala, also highly admired in Nicaragua. When the Quetzal flies, its long tail streams behind its shimmering blue-green body, making a motion that is almost serpentine. This observation by the Mayans and Aztecs led to the creation of the imagery and myth of the feathered serpent, Quetzalcoatl, who was a human king, the highest title for subsequent kings, who represents light, love, happiness and all which is good in life.

Quetzalcoatl represents the duality inherent in the human condition: the "serpent" is the physical body with its limitations,

---

35. (Yepes Boscan, 1996, pp. v-vi)
36. Night of Eve: Genesis 3:22-24; of Peter: Mark 14:66-72; of Judas: Matthew 26:47-56; Night of the Bridegroom: Matthew 25:1-13 (The New Open Bible Study Edition, 1990)
37. (Solis, Prologo a Poesia I, 2003, p. 350)

and the "feathers" are the spiritual principles. Quetzalcoatl is also the name in Nahuatl of the Meso-American Messiah and the title of the high priests of the Toltec religion. The last manifestation of Quetzalcoatl was King of Tula who lived between the years 947 and 999 of the Christian era. While Quetzalcoatl reigned, there were no human sacrifices.[38]

For PAC, Quetzalcoatl is a Christ figure. He explained to Steven White in an interview:

> 'When I wrote the Book of hours, this preoccupation began in me, which pursued me through practically all my work: to incorporate in my poetry the two traditions: Indian and Greek-Roman Spanish. Clearly, at the beginning with less knowledge and less experience, because one goes learning, deepening, assimilating this 'mestizaje', this fusion. But it seems to me that they are two very rich traditions that we have no reason to cut off, rather it is better to absorb them and give them in unity (as a whole) because we are, as mestizo, their synthesis...To speak Spanish we continue speaking Greek and Latin. The other is more difficult because it barely has language and is, besides, a challenge...that incites creativity and opens us to the mysterious zones of thinking and human feeling that the West has forgotten with its excess of rationalism. All these myths that are barely expressed in sculptures, in pottery; all these poems in embryo that one discovers in a petroglyph, in aboriginal rock art, in the drawing on a pot, are the words of mysterious content that still have not been formulated. One can have more freedom in creation with them...Nahuatl, above all, is very rich. It has many words that are like a bullet: they exploit an enormous charge of poetic creation...
>
> SFW: For example, what words?

---

38. Though one internet source says one sacrifice a year was required by Quetzalcoatl.

PAC: Well, I am going to cite one from the Nahuatl language: 'Quetzalcoatl.' Quetzalcoatl unites two words (like in the Greek), reality and dream, bird and serpent. That is to say, all philosophy and all myth, the highest humanist achievement of America, (fused) in the capsule of a word. It is as if we will fuse in one dual symbol Quixote and Sancho: reality and surrealist. [39]

Boscan in the section on 'Inculturation, poetry and theology,'of his Introduction to the Poetry of Pablo Antonio Cuadra's Book of Hours, explains that the Catholic Church incarnates the Gospel in diverse cultures and, at the same time, introduces those peoples, with their distinctive cultures and values, consolidates, perfects and restores them in Christ.' (Constitution Pastoral Gaudium et Spes, #58). The Church 'assimilates these values inasmuch as they are compatible with the Gospel in order to deepen the message of Christ...' Boscan views PAC as a:

'privileged spokesman for popular Latin-American religion capable of creating new, vital syntheses,'which is fruit of the encounter or cultural 'mestizaje' that he deliberately assumed and promoted in the modern culture of his country, and that the Church had already consecrated in the Pueblo Document. Admittedly, Bosco affirms, the Church by being open to so many different cultures, beliefs and philosophies worldwide could be vulnerable to strange and perplexing syncretism, though in Latin America the norm has been an obstinate link to the Christian God of the Bible. So PAC develops in his poetic thought the flowering of the true Latin American 'logos, ie. a 'mestizo logos, which is reason combined with emotion, eros, agape, myth and gratuity.' [40]

---

39. (White, <u>El Mundo Mas Que Humano en la Poesia de Pablo Antonio Cuadra: Un Estudio Ecocritico</u>, 2002, pp. 260-261)
40. (Yepes Boscan, 1996, pp. xviii-xx)

Another source from the internet stated that: 'Franciscans such as Toribio de Benavente "Motolinia" saw elements of Christianity in the pre-Columbian religions and therefore believed that Mesoamerica had been evangelized before, possibly by St. Thomas whom legend had it had "gone to preach beyond the Ganges". Franciscans then equated the original Quetzalcoatl with St. Thomas and imagined that the Indians had long awaited his return to take part once again in Gods kingdom.[41] Historian Matthew Restall concludes that:

> *"The legend of the returning lords, originated during the Spanish-Mexican war in Cortés' reworking of Moctezuma's welcome speech, had by the 1550's merged with the Cortés-as-Quetzalcoatl legend that the Franciscans had started spreading in the 1530's."*[42]

So the poet sees the myth of Quetzalcoatl, god and cultural hero of Mesoamerica, hybrid figure of bird-serpent, as the highest cultural construction of pre-Colombian poetic thought and contribution to formation of highest values of what it means to be American. The Aztecs expecting the return of their Quetzalcoatl probably believed he was the bearded foreigner with white skin who came from the sea prophesied by the Aztec seers. He appears in their chronicles as the wise, ascetic one who invented the calendar, a craftsman and mechanic, who became governor of his people and priest of a new religion. *'Lord who thought and invented himself,'* according to the Nahuatl text. His religious doctrine was a transcendent humanism that balances two forces that could be equally paralyzing: brute force on one hand and pure reason on the other.

---

41. Fray Francisco Ximenez in the introduction to the Mayan book, Popol Vuh suggests another conclusion: 'It is true that from the beginning (the Indian religions) began to speak of God and say things very similar to Holy Scripture and Catholic faith, aluding to what we know as revelation by the Holy Spirit; but I consider that these are found so mixed in a thousand lies and stories; one cannot consider these as Christian ideas, though without doubt they were inspirations to these Indians so that they lived in error, resulting so impure in relation to Catholicism, as is the source from which they proceed.' (Ximenez, 2005, p. 8)
42. Wikipedia

'This equilibrium', – writes Cuadra the essayist – *'man must achieve by penitence and self control. In all these texts is spoken of the prohibition of human sacrifices expressed by Quetzalcoatl. He is the prophet of a god of peace, not of war. His conception of God and of man opened to Mesoamerica the most fertile, extensive and peaceful cultural period of its history. As long as the influence of his doctrine lasted archeology proves the absence of vestiges of war and of defensive systems. None of the innumerable cities that flourished in this period were destroyed. Slowly abandoned, his memory remained indefinitely venerated in the following peoples and cultures.'*

But this wise and ascetic governor produced a counter-revolution of peace and brotherhood that did not sympathize with warriors. The Feathered Serpent offered mankind the freedom of wings and justice that permitted him to possess the land, in this way undermining the power of the strong and of the oppressors. *'In this way, Quetzalcoatl expresses antagonism to Power and War, and the myth, incarnating inconformity and resistance to the warrior castes and to the cruel 'teogonias' that demand human sacrifice, (which in turn) generated, against the humanistic reforms, the cultural hero figure of Tezcatlipoca or Necocyaotl, which in Nahautl means 'the sower of discords',... explaining the disgrace and fall of Quetzalcoatl.'*

From an interview with PAC, Steven White quotes the poet: *'... with frequency Tezcatlipoca has predominated, although in general, the majority of our people keep on hoping – and have struggled heroically for this hope – the return of the reign of Quetzalcoatl, although now the angels are those that announce him to the shepherds and indicate that where the true savior reclines his marvelous and divine humility is in a manger. ..faith in Quetzalcoatl as later faith in Christ were movements of conscience of great force resulting in pressing for rectifications and revolutions in our peoples. And I believe that this fire has not been put out. Blessedly. There is remorse when the light of the conscience is conserved aflame.'*[43]

---

43. (White, <u>El Mundo Mas Que Humano en la Poesia de Pablo Antonio Cuadra: Un Estudio Ecocritico,</u> 2002, p. 267)

PAC begins his 'Chapter' on Night and includes in the First Nocturnal poem descriptions of Quetzalcoatl, bringing up images of the serpent of Genesis, that beautiful creature who tempted Eve, leading to Adam's, and humanity's, fallen state and exile. PAC wrote from exile in Mexico, feeling that aspect of his mestizo heritage and identifying with the people whose myth involved this more complex understanding of the serpent.

PAC brings to mind Biblical nights where woman and man strayed from the best they knew, intimacy with God, to follow the lowest urgings of the serpent nature. Eve wanted her own way and the serpent promised that. In the darkest night, Peter out of fear three times denied knowing the One who he knew to be the giver of life. Judas sold his soul for silver in the night. These few examples are enough for every man and woman to recognize themselves as potentially capable of making the same dark choices that lead to the death of being cut off from God.

PAC mentions the night of the Bridegroom, from Jesus' words in Matthew 25, where the five virgins are ready for the coming of the Bridegroom and the five who were unprepared are left outside the joyous, light filled feast. That night comes when we do not expect it, and is related to the final night, the Apocalypse, of "revelation", the ultimate lifting of the veil in an era dominated by falsehood and misconception.

In the First Nocturnal poem PAC emphasizes Nicaraguan duality, which, universalized, is also human nature. The story of Jacob's wrestling with the angel includes the struggle of the known with the unknown, faith with doubt. He contrasts East and West, history with utopia thought with dream, logos against eros. On one hand there are night dreams and on the other hand there is the finality of death. There is the tension between the joyous wedding night and the terrors that are often associated with dark things done at night. There are the extremes between *'infinite joys'* and *'inexplicable frights.'* So PAC sets the stage for his poems on night.

It is interesting to note that there are eight poems related to the stages of Night, whereas Dawn, Morning, and Afternoon only have two or three poems each. Yet despite this imbalance, the poet made numerous revisions of his <u>Book of Hours</u> and those that remain are clearly his choice.

'*Tree of Night*' seems to be another poem to Mary, the Virgin, in the context of the angel who comes warning her of the fruit of the tree, the futility of the 'fruit of remembrance'. Mary rejects the forbidden fruit offered by the fallen angel, and does not go to the tree of the skulls of death. She kept her knowledge in silence. Within Mary grows the hope of the '*unexpected*,' '*you still carry the intact and the unknown*.' However, Steven White sees the 'counterdiscourse' aspect of the virgin as an unnamed Indian maiden who is '*Ixquic, mythical personage key to the Mayan culture in Popol Vuh*.'[44]

'*Exorcism of Shadows*' is written as a prayer of exorcism and protection, casting out lust, desolation, sickness, insanity, murder. The poet comes against '*the house of groaning,*' '*the wind of bitterness*', '*the discord of salt, the brothel and the well of the moon.*' All these are dispelled by the '*shadow of the Cross.*' And Mary, the brown skinned woman in silence receives cleanliness, rest, the peace of love, contentment in reality, full of delight to the Owner of the Word.

'*Flight to Egypt,*' the Second Nocturnal when night is darkest, refers to Joseph sold into slavery by his brothers' deception and then to Mary, exiled, carrying '*the infinite weight of a God in exile.*'

'*The Candle*' speaks of the blessedness of just a small candle lit in the darkness, welcoming the Visitor who brings '*sweet communication*' gathering around the Word.

'*Night above the Bridal Bed*' refers to Boaz and Ruth, who the poet pictures in Nicaraguan nights. A Nahuatl love poem is included to express even more exotically the comparison. The constellations seen in Nicaraguan nights move across the night skies like tropical birds, and the stories of Indian mythological gods are present above

---

44. (White, <u>El Mundo Mas Que Humano en la Poesia de Pablo Antonio Cuadra: Un Estudio Ecocritico</u>, 2002, p. 84)

the places where remembrances of Indian dances and lovers past repose restlessly, past and present. The poet identifies with both the Biblical persons and the Nicaraguan mysteries and realities.

'*Psalm of the Dark Night*' speaks to me of the dark night of the soul that is described by many Christian saints as the absence of feeling the Presence of God. Given that these poems were written in the conflict and upheavals of the poet's having to leave his beloved country and live in exile, there is added poignancy to the grief expressed. This is a prayer in which PAC is speaking to God, meditating on God's ways that have allowed this trouble. He expresses his anger, and reaching through the inability to understand, holds on by a thread of faith that continues to communicate, though as yet unanswered.

Finally is the '*Night of the Apocalypse*' which is three short poems all based on the darkness of the Book of Revelation.

I.   The City

II. The Horseman

III. The Lover, with the prophetic warning that all that seems normal in giving and receiving physical love is temporary, perishable, and will come to an end.

And so the poet closes his meditations on the <u>Book of Hours</u>, Dawn, Day, Afternoon, and the two watches of the Night, continues with the <u>Way of the Cross</u>, to conclude with the <u>Round of the Year</u>, a telling, from Nicaraguan experience, history and myth, the meaning of each month of the year.

BOOK OF HOURS

HYMN OF HOURS TO THE
EYES OF OUR LADY

I

Daughter of God the Father,
Purest Virgin before the birth
Into your hands I commit my faith
For you to illuminate.'

The eyes of Our Lady were blue in the Annunciation.
Since the first dawn.
since the first breezes, already gathered,
the color was ready. It was innocence,
the ineffable expectation of the first creatures
pronouncing the color of the Promise.

Since the faith of the larks, earlier still,
since the waters:
the Holy Spirit was moving over the surface of her eyes.
There was no air, there was no full moon
which upon divining the coming tenderness
would fail to sum up her blue. They sailed sustaining solitudes,
the nautical rose and the crystal origin of the seas.
All the blue of time, the voice of the prophets,
yielded color, virgin and miracle
because blue is happy. And light.

She was before the faraway.

Antecedent and victorious.

Since her infancy,
all the hours revolved reverently around her contemplation.
All the birds, heiresses of the ancients, again recognized
the accuracy of the first air.

Oh, heaven of sight, hail Mary:
veil of blue and faith so transparent
that the Lord is with you and You are blessed
among all the dawns your pupil sings!

The Archangel has come for your clean gaze,
the hummingbird has flown and the blackbird and the Scripture
and there is a loving air they cross announcing
eternal messengers.

We remember your blue in this song.
We receive the Light and open your window
to the valley, to the misty morning valley of our tears,
desiring to recover that gaze,
those first waters,
that blue certainty the archangels cross.

Return to us, those, your eyes,
where the cherubim, seated on your lashes
contemplate the silence of the Fish in the tranquil blue!

Let us, Lady, see with the faith of your gaze,
From see to see, our eyes might reach your distance!
They will go on drinking blue
reaching summits,
ascending to silences,
encountering Calendra larks and announcing angels
as from such height, doves and doves...!

II

'Mother of God the Son
Purest Virgin in the birth.
Into your hands I commit my hope
For you to nourish it.'

The eyes of Our Lady were green in Christmas.
Like the cedar that burns in the green flames of Lebanon,
like the slim cypress that pulses the wind of Zion,
like the palm that ascends and bursts its branches over Cadiz
like the rose of Jericho.
Like the spacious slow-blooded olive, sacramental and propitiatory.

Just like the bead-tree and the balsam,
like the aroma of tender vegetation
was your gaze, the fertile gaze of the earth!
Oh, Mother! Oh, most fruitful among the spring-times!
I hear the musical forests, I hear the wind
transporting the sweet sobs, the tenuous cry of the children.
Luminous Mother, happy processions of flowering wombs
traverse the grove of your eyes
and they go on singing the germinating song of morning:

God bless you, Mary, congregation of the wheat fields;
in your eyes the grape prepares its vintage
and within your mild gaze smiles the Lamb.
Blessed is your pupil tinged with hope
and blessed is the fruit of your womb, Jesus!

Bethlehem is the name of my infancy, adorned by
faraway elephants, mountain moss
and stars close at hand.

When we were innocent, we went with the sheep
and we saw in the gaze of your eyes fields in miniature.
The pines sang, Ah! We hailed the Infant!
We hailed the Tiny-God, the Prince of Presages,
the Preferred One!
Green paths led to Bethlehem!

Remember the little Indians entering on their knees
to your smiling eyes. We played with the ox.
And an Angel surveyed your pupil in flight,
lulling us to sleep with celestial fables and violins.

Then you sang lullabies for us
and you saw far away toward the future days
with your eyes damp like the fields with dew.

This is the gaze through which man returns to his hope!
Through here we depart, fortune on foot, to fugitive dreams.
We saw from Bethlehem other cities,
other stars
and distracted nights of untouched fullness.

Oh, the Autumnal nostalgia through your green gaze!
So many useless windows to look to the song,
to see the musical desire!
Open your eyes, oh, Mother of memory,
see me with Bethlehem, I want for my infancy!

III

'Wife of God the Holy Spirit,
Purest Virgin after the birth,
Into your hands I commit my charity
For you to inflame it.'

The eyes of Our Lady were black in the Passion;
black as though scorched by vast nights in flames,
black beneath love blowing inexpressible moans,
solitary eyes, victims in ashes of the burning grief!

From what remote weeping falls such affliction?...
Descended from Abel are the waters of lament,
and the pain of history passes through her eyes
like a funeral river in prolonged night!
I do not know if the wounded lily in the penumbra,
or the fatigued dove the wind tosses on the chill plain,
have that trembling of moans now spent,
or that impalpable dagger in the painful chalice of her breath
But there is a son who dies within her own blood,
and a brow that bows in the pain of her brow.
So many kisses kept only to fall wounded,
to nestle in lashes and dyed with martyrdom!
How many lullabies to rock his death
in the dread of a cold, halting rhythm!

Tell them, those who pass; those who have lost
the sweetness of a name on which to rest their lips,
tell them if there is pain sadder than her eyes
or color more bitter than her dark gaze!
Oh, deep of your eyes, Lady of death,
like night birds the darkness stalks

the pale cadaver that lies in your eyes!
Who can console the heaven that binds
the seas of your name? Horizons of outrage
have beset the dark waters of comfort!

Mother of affliction, crucified heart,
you have given in shadow the fruit of your womb
with the pain of blood of all women!

Let me in this song be seen in your eyes
and find that shadow where love resides
here, by the Cross exalted in your eyes!

Oh, painful Eve! Cut the fruit of the Tree
—the fiery apple that sprouts from the side—
my chest is with hunger! my chest is with you,
opened by sword!

DAWN

Capitulum

Midnight, cut by the edge of light (the light was created before the sun), an angelic and transparent air touches the water, ancient as the woman of Zacharias, grandmother water Mother of the earth, and moves in her womb a powerful newness. Necessary life. Creator Time. Something is born —Matins[1]— and scales the levels of the dream until the rooster's song. This one beats his wings, yet does not fly, but sings. Because poetry is detained by death.

Thus, day is prophesied on the Vespers[2] of its creation. Afterward the Angel of Heaven[3] will come to recreate its possessions. And in the dawn will begin, quotidianly,[4] hope.

---

1.   *Matins* – (Earliest of the canonical hours in the Catholic Church.)
2.   *Vespers* – (The sixth of the seven canonical hours; evensong.)
3.   *Patria* – (Native country, place of birth, home, or Heaven.)
4.   *quotidianly* – (Occurring on a quotidian basis; daily or commonplace.)

Antiphony of the Dreamer

From blood we are awakening.
We have woven the last dreams. We make garlands
between dreams. The fresh sheets receive you,
Oh, announcement! Oh, promise! Oh, serene hope!
                              —The roosters are singing.

We do not waken. There is no light to survey
the first wheat sprigs, the damp little flowers
born to the bramble. We are as though supposing
that our hands touch sweet flowers.
                              —And the dew is falling.

No. This song does not pass in the sound.
I am still so far! I have shadow.
But there is a slow trance that evaporates death from this dream.
This is light even before its name.
                              —Just its feeling.

Chorale of the Poets of the Dawn

Resurrexit sicut dixit Alleluia!

Ah! Now the world has begun to turn!
The four winds have made swirl the perfumes that reposed.
The perfume of the moon has been spilled on the udders,
on the breasts of woman it has been spilled.
The perfume of the solitary star has moved in the roses,
on the lips of the maidens it has smiled.
The perfume of silence has surveyed the word,
on the voice of poets it has flowered.

Go to the men who ask for their horses,
the men who give voice in the sheets of the dawn.
Ah! the horses were just formed and the new paths.
All the animals, all the elements have encountered their newness.
This is the hour we recognize the infancy of the little boy,
this is the hour of the tenderness of the calf.
The hour that is bleating, singing, huddling.
The women just arrived, the early risers, to the nest of the angels.
The women now return, the early risers, with freshly washed faces,
with the drops of the morning on the birth of their hair.
'Heaven —they have said— is the sweet country of light.'
Men have mounted their horses and they set out to their age.
They spend their years on the move.

We go with the light up to our waist, we go splashing.
We know that happiness is a sum of auroras.
We have drunk the wine of the morning,
in the corrals, in the stables we have drunk the juice of the dawn.

We are the new men!

National Hymn
(on the eve of light)

At the limits of the dawn my small country drinks the waters spread out,
the great naked waters that rest.
'I will make lagoons this day,' it thinks. Counting, two by two,
/its trees,
its villages covered with dew,
its territories that go slowly out in the night.
Before man, even before roosters
my sweet country arranges its portion of landscape:
'I will place this blue over a new woman,'
'this place I project for better winds' —it goes saying.
This land precedes you, men of my earth!
The dawn pulses, pulses other nostalgias to seek the angel
that circulates from dream to dream around our airs.
My little country, among so many, goes historifying its flowers,
the complex biography of the swallow,
dates of Ceibo trees, of rabbits,
stories of rebellious men, other destinies
in a spring, in a district barely surveyed.
There are countries that chose laborious calendars
to eclipse the ancient writings.
Let it be called Empire, the pain of some faraway men.
It will be called 'Immortal', a name cast against the bronze.
But behold, this place exists willing to be eternal
by the one word that an angel dictates, watching over the Matins.
My little country is inhabited by less solemn vegetation,
by natural silences that move from song to song,
among that kind of men, among mountains prone to weep
and prudent rivers that gently transport their stars!
Here we have raised forgotten elementals to be common,
insistent vegetation to cover our footprints to time.

And there is an angel that repudiates our opportunities
—Close with insolence the sordid windows of the merchants!—
and comes urging one more word, one more song
in the poor village that does not transcend,
inhabited by this pale boy that we did not know.

Thus the dawn takes the thread to the dream from the birds
and goes penetrating all those inscribed in its silence.
(My little Christian country is composed of some few Spring-times
/and belfries,
of mockingbirds, short trains and boy sailors).
'We have this chore, this word among us,' it has said,
and so it begins, on the verge of the dawns, crying
unto you, sapphire, called the last star,
unto the deer, the Güis, the Chichitote —an early rising bird—
its chorus of clarity to praise the light.
I survey so many, calling those who have earned their silence:
To you, José Muñoz, carpenter by trade, who knows how to make
/my table,
take this star. In comes out to guide your hour. Put it together!
And you, Martin Zepeda, well, you go walking, rustle
these birds. Give them song or tell them
what you know of bread and the guitar.
And to you, Pedro Canisal, cowboy, rustic youth:
saddle the horizon, ride to the end of the night, tame it!
Everyone dream. Everyone show that you are with me
making this future day, svelte and without anguish.
I search for Juan, 'el Chato,' in this neighborhood of bricklayers,
For Gumersindo, day laborer of roads:
I have a wide space to fill
from Chontales to León, from North to river, from river to heart.
This, your voice, Gregorio Malespín, singer from Cuiscoma:
Get up!
See the people that go with me. They are already singing:
lakes, lagoons, mother forests
trees and campesinos say: 'Praised be the Just
and Good Lord who gives to each country its own:
this night to ours.
This rest achieved.'

For so much,
in praise and deserved song,
trees and country-folk say: ' Praised be the Owner
of this possession. He lifted one more night and walked
on, to cover another place of greater need.'
For thus, we thank this place, as we should.
Thus, we live again, in our place, as we should.
My little country solicits you for the prayer and the hymn of those
                                        /of us who will wake.
Remember, brother, the hills of Colojá and its green grass.
You, Jacinto Estrada, rejoice in your island
with its fruit trees the bees whisper around.
Mother of mine, from the balcony of your house bless my
                                        /respiration!
While I dream of a song where it goes on building,
all this county's rhythm of celestial angels and green palms,
rocked, from port to starboard, by a wind of slow flutes.

MORNING

Capitulum

After the water, the air, Grace-gift of the day.

The diphthongs of the bells gallop. It is the virgin hour of the Annunciation. Birds and towers. Messengers. Elemental time of bread and wine. Of wheat and of the word 'new'.

In the rural rites, the laborers recognize the first sweat, brother of the ear of grain. Fructifying Sun.

Morning is of the Spirit. 'Lumen Cordium.'

Matutinal Antiphony

Heaven is a vessel of purest crystal.
Think on this morning
that you guard in your pupil full of wonder:
study the birds it cages, scrutinize
its burnished blue
and name it.
Call her Inez
or Agate.

Matutinal Chorus of the Laborers

Song for the dance of the wheat:
Shout of gold.

                                    Triumphant Plant!

Subtle arrow of bread. Vegetal
sword in the door of paradise.

                                    Wheat!

Glade of wheat: scepter in the hand of Power.
Embroider the celestial tunic: needle of cereal.
Embroider the mantle of the sun.

                                    Wheat!

Inflame the hunger of the new mystery
Kill the hunger of the terrestrial. Liberate wheat!
Scepter in the hand of Love:

                                    Triumphant plant!

Invitation to the vagabonds

*'Then their eyes were opened
and they recognized him.'*

Luke 24:31

Towers
Tall pastors of day.
Cowbells of celestial metal, bells
for us, vagabonds,
flocks from the broken sheep-fold and solitary
that we saw burn the matutinal star.

To those who no one had gathered, they called:
—'Go out to the roads and fences
and impel how many you may find.'

—'You who do not know yourself: you are our brother.'
And they asked the walker:
—'Where lies the hut of the orphans?'
and to the boatmen who rise early upon the waves:
—'Give us the route of the island of the blind.'

I heard on the dock the voices of the fishermen
And the shudder of the matutinal sails.
'Where is the cliff where the widow of the navigator weeps?'
And to the cattle driver of long shouts imbibed of horizon:
—'Loan us your horse to rescue the lost.'

Towers
Archangels of stone.

Voices for the sons of inaccuracy and fatigue:
the wounded, the sad, those who suffer
persecution by justice.
—'We have seen —they said— words fall in ruin,
that laboriously we elaborate to name our dreams.'

This they said.
Because the vagabonds were arriving,
Because they were the disabused and the fugitives;
the exiled who announced the blessed insurrection of poverty;
and there were men of ebony segregated in their nocturnal reigns;
pastors of distant eyes
that numbered the legendary trees in whose shadow they slept.

And we saw the poet with his inadmissible suit of melancholy;
and we watched the blind man with his floating step and his hands
in search of an untouchable horizon;
and the cripple jumping over his invisible obstacle
and the soldier who is a beggar of more recent wounds
—'We have already given too many dead to the irresolute questions
we looked to one side and another, and our fathers,
and the fathers of our fathers
opened holes in the earth to bury their names,
to sow them in the hope of producing his new name,
a pronounceable name and not anonymous, indelible, memorable,
/respectfully exalted.
Long centuries they buried their humiliated names,
long centuries they died, and long centuries they fertilized the parched
/earth,
but death only produced silence and oblivion accumulated
/new oblivions,
and interrogations grew back above the tombs
and questions over the sepulchers
and once again hope is an ambush
and happiness once again a future
that should be constructed with new innumerable new sepulchers.'

This they said,
And the bells hushed.

Who was the last vagabond to return from the night?
We saw his long shadow advance over the dust
and wake the flowers with tremulous drops of dew.

Perhaps you have heard the beggar when he says:
'Shall I call Night the inauguration of my sorrows.'?
Has it reached your song, the voice of the exiled that murmurs:
'Is my obligation to leave called nation'?

Such was the last beggar.
And those who saw him arrive,
believed to hear in his silence what they did not hear in words.
We saw unknown men place before his fatigue,
interrogations in sweetly strange languages.
Fishermen accustomed to the deep
expected from his lips what they had never expected from the
/lips of the sea

And we saw the eyes of the prostitute
uneasy and humble.

And one to another said:
—'Who is the last beggar?'
and one and another returned to him and asked:
—'Tell us, what must we do with our thoughts?'
And he would be silent.
And we saw him advance to the table,
put down his worn staff, open his knapsack
and upon taking the bread and breaking it
our eyes were opened.

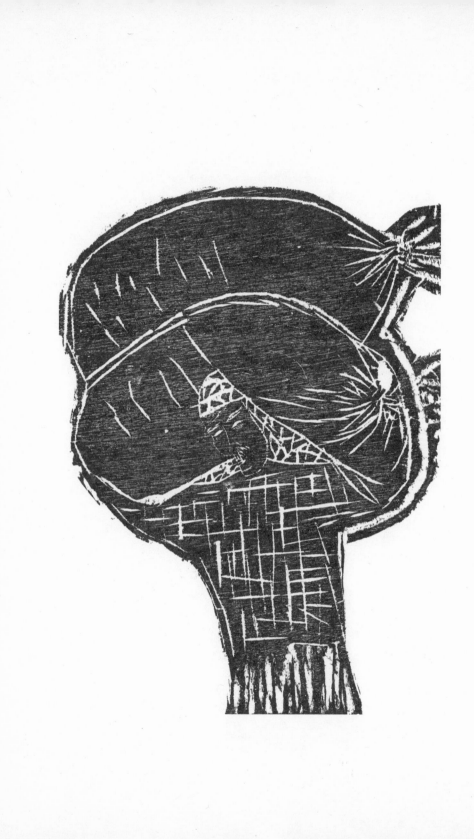

AFTERNOON

Capitulum

Fire: essence of mid-day.

Afternoon runs burning from the hour of the crucifixion[5] to the hour of the descent. The clock of the Cross gives its hour of blood. Hour of martyrs. Hour of the scream, because the Word[6] has been pierced.

But after the fire, the heart and the return still remain. The Vesper star whistles to the flocks, and from distant horizons of twilight they come to the only Shepherd.[7]

Church[8] and Judgment.[9]

---

5. The crucifixion was at midday, the sixth hour, 'Luke 24:44. The 'Sext' hour, noon, was one of the canonical hours, or offices of prayer.
6. '...And the Word became flesh, and dwelt among us, and we beheld His glory...' John 114
7. Jesus said, 'I am the good shepherd, and I know My own and My own know Me.' John 10:14
8. 'Christ also is the head of the church. He Himself being the Savior of the Body.' Ephesians 5:23
9. 'Faithful and True; and in righteousness He judges and wages war;... and His name is called 'The Word of God...King of Kings and Lord of Lords...' Revelation 19:11-16

Chorale Hymn of the instruments of the passion

'O Crux, ave, spes, unica...'

The death of the seed began in the furrows.[10]
Its renewal burned in the desperate light of the blood.
You were calling.
You were writing, oh scarlet letter![11]
writhing your arms like a tree that has lost his birds.
You were marking with fire the afternoon of the world.
Rise up, detractors! Sow discord! This is your hour!
Who has raised their plant above this earth at knife point?
What beggar tree, ragged vegetal, grows in your silence?

And she affirmed her age, the great mother Ceiba
secular and slow with the testimony of wood:
'I know the biography of a tree —she said—;
his powerful genealogy in the vegetation of mystery,
his indefatigable paternity from seed to seed.
I know a priestly tree, heir of prayer
and of the hands that implore,
whose branches have elevated his cry above the swords.
I know a tree at whose right hand an angel has grown,
daily lifting his stature.
His knotted hands excavate beneath the Testament[12],

---

10. *Furrows - '...if it dies, it bears much fruit.'* (John 12:24)
11. *The Scarlet Letter* - Jesus, the 'Alpha and Omega', first and last letter of the Greek alphabet, beginning and end. (Revelation 22:13) Jesus is the Tau cross written with blood of the Passover Lamb on the doorposts so the death angel would pass over. (Exodus 12:1-14)
12. *'Testament'* – both Old and New Testaments in the Bible. First appears the Tree of Knowledge in Genesis guarded by an angel in Paradise. At the end of the Bible, in Revelation, appears the tree of Life, whose leaves are for the healing of the nations.

because the roots cross all memory
and all man has forgotten.'

Then rose up metal from the great brother Iron
        —initiated in the mystery of blood—
and tore out his shout, his penetrating structure.
'Sing, tongue —he said—
sing the virtue of the saving timber,
sing the solicitude of wood
and his buoyant mercy for the ship-wrecked.
Every ship sings; the Ark[13] that safe-harbors in the iris,
the faithful incense vessel upon the waves
where we go crowded,
uncomfortable and brothers,
protestants of the wind or wise opposers of the route;
sing the navigating Church[14]
the rudder in the hands of the weary fisherman,[15]
his bloodied solitary mast: cross of tempest and of courage.'

And rose up the sad, flagellant, Brother Lash
        —the strident equator that girds the weak air—
and in moaning junctures their thin members
sang: 'Oh Cross,
vulture through the ages,
eternal bird of the high abyss,
insatiable devourer of death!
Who surveys summits,
who nestles in a dying kiss,
in the disconsolate breast,

---

13. *Ark and rainbow/ iris* – Noah's ark symbol of God's promise of protec-
    tion. (Genesis 9) 'Iris' in Spanish is the colored part of the eye, from
    the three poems to the eyes of Our Lady at the beginning of the Book of
    Hours.
14. *uncomfortable and brothers* - all the churches who follow Christ and
    would be counted as believers ie. Protestants as well as Roman Catho-
    lics.
15. *Fisherman* – Peter, disciple of Jesus, head of the Church, fishers of men.
    (Matthew 16:18, Matthew 4:19)

in the hard wall hostile against weariness?
I want your wing-stroke in the shout of certainty
bird of the Great Council,
flight of resurrection,
I want your resonant cry in the zenith: ſ
'Woe! Woe! Woe! are they that inhabit over the earth!';
your inexpressible groan,
oh, feathered Cross,[16] brooder of the world,
warm, merciful, gathering your chicks,
celestial Jerusalem!

Up rose the piercing, disinherited voice,
sister Bramble —rustic epileptic—,
dragging her ruined vegetal.
'I ask for a star —she said—, I ask in its drop of firmament
for your luminous compass.
Epiphany[17] of the astral rose —sign of the great King.
May your illumination appear over the house of the humble,
may the unexpected man rejoice in your luminary,
stellar magic of bread,
guide of the dawn, oh! brooch of the horizon,
constellation of happy tears.
Fire of sword!'

And rose up sister Gall of Bitterness
and Laughter and Saliva from the shadows:
'We know —they said— that this tree is born of the mouth of men.
We know that this tree grows from the silence of the dead.
We know that its fruit is the heart: apple of misery!'[18]

---

16. *Feathered Cross* – Jesus wept before entering the city: *'I wanted to gather your children together, just as a hen gathers her brood under her wings, and you would not have it!'* (Luke 13:34)
17. *Epiphany* - January 6, the coming of the Magi as the first manifestation of Christ to the Gentiles. (Webster, 1977)
18. *Apple of misery* –in Genesis, fruit of the knowledge of good and evil, fruit of death.

Then the Man rose up, guilty and savior.[19]
Man against himself —in his agony and glory—,
laurel and thorn upon his cursed brow,
executioner of his dream
and God of his nostalgia:
'Cross is my cradle, scaffold of the first cry —he clamors—
Cross, the love of the body, gallows of joy.
Cross, the bed where everyday agony lies.
I am my punishment hanging from the tree by my arms.
Nail my hand, the touch, tempting and prisoner.
Nail my feet on the insatiable routes
the weight, the time, the body on the cross,
and here nailed to this summary
—to the more and more of death—, I am the life.
Cross is this rupture of self in earth and heaven.
Cross, this love that comes out of the hands to the level of the
/maidens,
or that is elevated from weeping to the height of the angels.
Cross because a man has been nailed in my desire.
Cross because a God has been crucified upon my body!'

When the Man said his last word,
the darkness and shadows were lifted.
All creatures were in the chalice of darkness,
All creatures were of the lineage of shadows.
'Listen!' —they said— We have been constructed in the likeness
/of this tree,
and every creature's flower was marked by his sign!
The vertex of the winds sings his sign,
the union of the elements, and the cross-roads!
Every bird that spreads its wings to sustain the song of its route
Every gathering of stars over the four points of destiny
Every man extended for love
commemorates the impassible balance of your judgment:
Oh, blessed support! Oh, fertile equilibrium! Oh, faithful Cross!'[20]

---

19. *Savior* - Jesus is the Son of Man, the new Adam, innocent and Savior.
20. *Oh Faithful Cross* –the Creator's mark of the Cross in every creature and
aspect of creation.

Christ in the Afternoon

It was when the decay of the poppy.
When the precipitated senescence[21] of the violet.
In that place. At the door of the nocturne temple,
where Mother Afternoon, hoary, leaning on her weariness,
left in the money box her only coin.[22]

                                                    In that hour.

Calling from Emmaus, from other afternoons,
from indelible beaches, from villages:
See that I reunite in the heart all things that restore.

I call, I convoke in this hour the faces that return
with a coat of time —some hours demolished—
over the brilliant youth of the morning
See that I call to the ports, plead to the seashore
where the navigators return, damp with sea,
still brimming from their fluvial labors.
The lodging-houses,
the hanging nests,
the tall pendular palms of the golden orioles,
the yawning caves of the fox and the margay:
every place of refuge, I carry it with me now sweetly
receiving memories,
receiving the songs of arrival.

I am reuniting the awaited steps,
the happy approach of the returning
—mothers who peer at their own pupils, questioning,

---

21. *Senescence* – Biological aging after maturity. (Wikipedia)
22. *Coin* - The widow's mite, offering that Jesus approved. (Mark 12:43)

featherless mockingbirds that chirp, suckling puppies,
and those that I have pronounced with preference
because their return is withered with solitude—.
Ah! I have come. I have arrived with them.
See that I accompany one by one so much outcome.
See the breast being opened, welcoming you in,
painfully torn for your afternoon rest.
See that I call.

      It is my voice that carries this transient bird.
There it sounds: in the rose on the verge of cancelling its
                              /exposition,
in that hand of the father slowly sliding across the son's brow,
in the prudent fire of bread,
in the warmth of the beloved who once again gives refuge.
I am daybreak and nightfall!
For you who see the sun descend and are devoured by the silence
—dispossessed from the crepuscular, travelers without return—
this is the hour in which I have been descended to my setting.
They lower my body with yours
and I share with you my last afternoon.

Oh, come! I have emptied of blood my heart
to make room for men to recline their grief!

NIGHT

Capitulum

Night is of the earth.

Serpent that crawls in its exile, seeking the complementary Quetzal of auroral plumes. Night like weeping in this valley of tears. Night in the sinister of the dream. Left of death. Silence of the great struggle, night of weddings and of agonies. Of infinite joys and inexplicable frights.

Night of Eve, of Peter, of Judas, of the sinner. Night of the arrival of the Groom: 'media nocte clamor jactus est...'[23]

Night or Apocalypse.

---

23. Night of Eve: Genesis 3:22-24; of Peter: Mark 14:66-72; of Judas: Matthew 26:47-56; Night of the Bridegroom: Matthew 25:1-13

The struggle with the angel (First nocturnal)

When I arrived to the limit of the night
—between the blue of Abel and the blue of Cain—
to this limit that divides you
between your past and your future,
I —Jacob— was left alone.
And I saw a man. Was it I or was it the other?
And this man struggled with me
until the aurora shone.
I struggled with myself and I knew
the strength of the Unknown.
He struggled against me and I knew
the resistance of the Known.
Was it, perhaps, Faith
insistent on removing Doubt?
Was it Orient and its gilded
pavilions against the purple livid
Occident in flames? Was it, perhaps
History plunging its foot in the sand
against the power of Utopia?
Or was it your Thought
detaining your Dream, or Logos
against Eros? Oh, tell me your name
dark angel. Tell me
who I am. Tell me
Prince of the Itzas,
'am I this that I am?'
because I have looked back —on my right—
and I have heard my brothers
guided by the Omens
since Quetzalcoatl left Tula toward exile.
And I have looked back —on my left—

and I have heard my brothers
guided by the Promise
since Abraham left his country
and undertook the paths of Exodus.

Tell me your name, you who struggle with me.
Is your name Mayan or is it Greek,
is it Nahuatl or Roman? Do you come
from the sea or are you aboriginal?
Tell me your name, I beg of you.
But the other, seeing that he did not prevail
struck me in the thigh,
And the Known
was supplanted by the Unknown.
And in my failure I found my success.
And never again could I, triumphant,
recover my triumphant step.

The tree of the night

You are virgin and the angel detains you
at the foot of the tree of night.

Distance yourself, girl, from the dark descendant
carbonized by the dream.
I warn of impossible things.
I warn of solitary fruits,
livid lips that know humiliating secrets,
closed eyes,
eyelids,
fallen on tedium, eternally the same.
Old, dark moons rot their serenades,
impregnating the air with a scent of time.

Forbidden to you is the fruit of remembrance!
Do not come to the tree where the skulls hang.
I warn of the face of the fugitive;
the vain lip whose words you rejected;
the hostile moon that wove your silence by the sea.
You still possess the unexpected.
You still carry the intact and the unknown.

If you are virgin, do not look in the eyes from whose hung
                                    /criminals exude fatigue,
do not hear the voices loosed from Autumn most ancient,
do not touch the hands that balance
weary of groping infinite walls!

Exorcism of the shadows

I exorcise the black bee that sips in the West.
    The blushing flower of desire is its tribute.
    In the Bride-chambers, in the silence of the ocotales, it
                          /finds its desolation.

I exorcise the hidden flint of the storm.
    Yellow cholera is its territory.
    In the dark bends, cowardly, flings its saliva.

I exorcise the serpent of smoke, girdle of the night.
    The pallor of insanity is its home.
    In the restless dreams, in the treacherous sounds
                      /it opens its rings.

I exorcise the dishonest scarab of iron rust
    the crow blackened by eclipses.
    the flying sorrow of the owl, custodian of assassins.

I exorcise the house of moans.
I exorcise the wind of bitterness.
I exorcise the ashes, the discord of salt,
    the brothel and the well of the moon.
Three times I cite against you the sign of nightfall.

Against your shadow I cite three times the shadow of the Cross:
    Against the temptation of the woman enlightened by the star.
    Against the ambush of the dagger impelled by ire.
    Against the step of the phantom covered by lime.

May this shadow prepared the rest
    be clean.

May this shadow prepared for love
      be a dove.
May this shadow prepared for illusion
      be a smile.

May it be holy and innocent, the creature night.
Open, brown woman, your rose of oblivion into the hand of the
                                      /Angel.
May your silence be delightful to the Owner of the Word.
                                 Be!

The flight to Egypt (Second Nocturnal)

In the nights of the desert
When things passed again through your heart
or the fear
and the stars spoke to you
of the immense Power that covered you,
but the bird that shrieked
was not an angel, nor the leopard
nor anguish, nor the ancient wind
with the laments of the Mangled and the strange
force of the Evil of Mizraim or the fist
of the King like the cloud
of torment threatening on the horizon;
when you thought —meaning to free him
from his brothers— on the Dreamer
sold in Dothan and, following his tracks,
you feared beneath the palm tree
the noise of the night, the hushed
treaties of the wicked or the lurking beast
and the face, the unrecognized face, of hatred
over innocence, oh, Exiled one!,
did you hear,
it came to you, just, like the wind
that increases at the coming out of the moon,
the prayer of your children? Thousands of lips,
thousands of years, of men, thousands
of mothers and exiles
and fears and nights and the same strange
force of evil and the starry
heaven, did you hear the cosmic
murmur, the stellar weight over
your mother's shoulders? Ah!

Did you feel that firmament was
your heavy mantle
and to grow over your arms
to grow the infinite
weight of a God in exile?

The candle

Outside
—among the shadows—
we hear the steps
of the Visitor.

The industrious
and syndical bee
offers the substance
of this flame:
        light of the poor.
The honey burns.
The sweet communication
is inflamed.
We gather
around the Word.
Oh, night! *Oh vere
beata nox*!

Nocturne over the bridal bed

The Nicaraguan nights produce sweet certainties in the unstable
/heart.
Boaz, the sower, descends toward the valleys.
He comes from the Bible and crosses the white
dunes of the Way of Santiago. It is magnificent
his chest of bucolic maturity. Nicaraguan nights
produce strange delights and fascinations:
timid women ignite suddenly fireflies
in their pupils
and from their wombs fall sighs to the womb of the earth:
then wings are born to the ants and they fly their
nuptial flights.
The gleaner reclines in the Southern window.
Long black locks
sway the winds of ebony.
Now the beloved nears, beneath the poplar grove.
'Zacuán papalotl con ya chichina'
(Yellow butterfly sips the honey.)
'¡Xochitl cueponqui!'
(The flower has opened!)

Ruth invokes the moon
And spreads the white sheets over the Bridal bed.
The Nicaraguan nights produce strange fascinations and delights:
Practical men, made of coarse prose, ferment the corn
and hear sing within the grain, the rooster of merriment;
Indians, solemn as princes,
lift their foot in the air and spin around the cadenced females
as spin the stars and the hours in their musical orbits.
In the Nicaraguan nights, girls, in a bird's age, begin their first
/flights

and fall, breast pierced by darts and poems,
not to the earth, but to the deep blue country of the angels.
This night Boaz has the heavens between his arms.
The heavens and their boisterous
swarm of constellations. The reddish
look of Aldebarán Yohualtecutlí, burning
in bed like the female leopard.
The celestial pupil of Citalmina
(she who shoots arrows of contempt).
Or the lachrymose
diamond of Venus Hueicitlalli, the sweet
procurer of reconciliations.
The sower has looked into the unfathomable eyes of my race
the first night of the world, oh, night of Tuxtla!
Rainy night of Copán! Has seen the gleaming
eye of Iztac Mixcóatl, the white serpent that crosses the black heavens
laying the eggs of the dreams of men.
Beloved! —says the poet— repose on my breast your night of
/dark eyelids!
Beloved! —she says— outside I hear the wind groan, tethered and
/conjugal.
…In the full moon the navigators turned their eyes
and saw in the domain of the moon
the Bridal bed of lovers.
Igneous angels came and went
bearing honey.
They came and went.

Psalm of the dark night

Night is ancient and reserved.
Dark angels keep watch, muting the communion of words.
Where will I find a response —oh, solitude!— to the cry of the
                                        /abandoned?
Wounded I go, Lord, among your invisible vineyards.
Like a blind man I perceive the dark murmur of your wheat fields.
Night is the veil of your Glory and I go crossing its captivity.
Who is that angel that now strums my blood with his slow hand?
I would walk through a land almost prosperous
You had told me it was worth more than a great number of birds.
And I had loved the Earth and acquired the name of its things.
But you have thrown down my flesh upon the rock.
That colt that flees feels the fright still
And those that accompanied me looked at me with sadness and
                                        /now have gone!
This is the end of those that have followed your path
Oh! Why do lovers deceive themselves and still endure?
You have flung me from my delight to submerge me in a thirst that
                                        /nothing satisfies.
I believed I could trust in the hand you extended me
And you placed my hand where it has forever been pierced!
If you would stay with me I would be nourished in your presence
But you have abandoned me in the place of your execution
And you only want me to perceive the darkness of my sin.
Hard it is to love according to your conditions!
Hard is the earth when you place this implacable sword in its
                                        /portals!
See how I return —alone among such neglect!— from knowing
                                        /man,
With side opened, springing from crepuscules that redden my
                                        /vesture.

In vain I survey the walls of your silence like a wintry beggar.
I have hurled my shouts against the nocturnal angels!
Like a blind man I have beaten with fists the darkness of your
                                                    /sanctuary!
I ask not that this path cease, whose distance I have lost with
                                                    /my blood.
I ask for a night less deep for these helpless eyes!

Night or the Apocalypse

I. The City!

' And they shouted upon seeing the smoke of its burning...'

(Revelation 18:18)

Judgment or crepuscule, your blood
poisons the sea.
Raise your slow smokescreen,
oh, night, and such heart,
such efficacy
       and things
sweetly infinite that burn!
Civilizations that give one day
to the great fire.
       And a rose
that alone is enough.

...Raise your slow smokescreen,
oh, night!

II. The horseman

'Because the power of horses is in the mouth...'

(Revelation 9:19)

I dismounted the archaic potro[24] blackened by the fire.
The wind stiffened its mane
tempestuous
like choleric bouquets of serpents.

(Great shouts stained with vultures
the lunar wall where the ocean churned!)

...I also had been a horseman,
had charged against the names
marked by the blood!

I also spilled bitter chalices
and there are traces on virgin lips painfully indelible
where the Horseman ignited his splendor and then departed
/under the night...

---

24. *potro* – colt; a wooden frame for shoeing unruly horses; torture rack

III. The lover

'And they have no rest...'

(Revelation 14:2)

On the banks of the night
the scholastic multitude of lovers
universal and silent...

Like blind teachers
the cavillous stars interrogate man
and smile ancient
to the passionate repetition.

(Oh,
the infinite murmur
of hands
drawing women in the night!)

...But they will pass the sponge
over the cold satiety of the dawn
because everything perishable was written!

INTRODUCTION

TO PABLO ANTONIO CUADRA'S
WAY OF THE CROSS

by Sarah Hornsby

The marginalization to which Cuadra had been submitted for his independent line of thought and his religious faith, besides the national situation of repression and war, caused him to be bound to the Christ of Calvary —without losing by this his Christian optimism— facing the cruel and Inquisition-like dominance of the 'constructors of paradises.' [1]

Pablo Antonio Cuadra wrote the Fourteen Stations of the Way of the Cross in the midst of the disillusionment with the Sandinista Government after the Triumph of the Revolution. *'My commitment with the Revolution —he declared in 1982—, is to always be on the side of the Nicaraguan People, for their constant liberation, for their fundamental rights, for their hopes. Not on the side of Power, not on the side of the 'formulas' nor of the grand words, but (on the side) of Man. I believe that is my obligation as Poet and as Christian.'* [2]

At an early age PAC was nourished and trained in the spirituality of the Jesuits in Managua. Under the shadows and green fernlike fronds of flamboyant trees and tropical mango trees, he dedicated days and weeks to the Spiritual Exercises of Ignatius of Loyola. These studies challenged the follower of Jesus to identify everyday life with the events and actions of Jesus, as the Word, the expression of God in Person. [3] In many of his poems Biblical themes

---

1. (Solis Cuadra, 2008, pp. 152-153)
2. (White, El Mundo Mas Que Humano en la Poesia de Pablo Antonio Cuadra: Un Estudio Ecocritico, 2002, p. 264)
3. (Guardia, 2004, 2007, pp. 2-3)

are identified with everyday life in Nicaragua. The path that led
Jesus to the cross, shown in fourteen steps, is PAC's identification
of the Nicaraguan situation, *'following behind the way of the cross
- humanity that has suffered passion and death.*[4]

The Way of the Cross was written with compelling images
that only a poet could write. PAC uses convincing narration
which only a journalist could write. He creatively interweaves
our everyday, ordinary experience in family, neighborhood, nation
with the whole of creation, cosmic and Scriptural history and truth.
PAC writes like no others I know because his Via Crucis

• is infused by the Holy Spirit and rings true.

• illumines what is often made dull from repetition or made
saccharine sweet from spiritualizing the very earthy,
bloody, torturous, painful reality beyond the mind's
comprehension.

• inspires with his succinct yet commanding visualizations
of the persons surrounding Jesus' Passion, enabling the
reader to identify with those persons and have the courage
to receive the healing those wounds offer, and walk that
road with the cross that Jesus gives each of us individually
and as a body of believers.

When we came to Nicaragua in 1984, we were introduced
to the other side of the experience of a people still at war, the ones
Reagan called 'the epitome of evil.' Invited to begin Habitat for
Humanity in Nicaragua by CEPAD, an ecumenical Protestant
Alliance of churches also supported by the Presbyterian World
Mission Board, we saw the realities of Nicaragua through glasses
darkened by shame that our great nation, the United States of
America, was seen here as the Imperialists, compared to the Roman
Empire of Jesus' day. It was our government that was financing the
Contras, who were headed by the dreaded Somoza National Guard,
who had been schooled in 'our' School of the Americas. Politicized,
some called us, though friends and fellow missionaries took us to see

---

4.   (Cuadra P. A., personal letter, 1966)

many different aspects of Nicaragua's war-time reality, including a visit to La Prensa, the newspaper directed by Pablo Antonio Cuadra censured and closed by the Sandinistas. We did not meet PAC, because he was in self-exile, teaching Central American Literature at the University of Texas in Austin.

After the two year Habitat for Humanity Project in rural German Pomares, Chinandega, was completed, on a typical scorching hot day, in a caravan raising clouds of dust, dignitaries came to dedicate the houses we had built. Jim, Matthew and I hosted President Jimmy and Rosalynn Carter, chauffeured by Nicaragua's President, Daniel Ortega and his wife, Rosario Murillo, along with Miguel de Escoto, Priest and Minister of the Exterior (later President of the United Nations); Sergio Ramirez, Vice-President; and Miguel Ernesto Vigil, Minister of Housing. Lunch was served under our thatched roof shelter and the women made a chop-suey lunch over an open fire. I was a nervous wreck! The multitude of press and body guards was served an improvised meal at the site of the house dedication. Daniel Ortega willingly gave a Bible to each of the new home owners, although at least one U.S. based Protestant ministry was raising funds to smuggle Bibles into Nicaragua!

Before coming to Nicaragua, the only news we had of the place where we would live for two years was a photo of a Russian tent hospital. The general opinion of Ronald Reagan, widely accepted by many of our family, was that the Sandinistas were the enemy of mankind. The Sandinistas also held that opinion of the United States. After our brief training in Americus at Habitat Headquarters, Director and Founder, Millard Fuller took us for a visit to the Carter's home in Plains. Jimmy Carter promised to dedicate the first one hundred houses we built as a symbol of good will from North Americans. He loaned us a book by the ousted dictator of Nicaragua, Somoza, written in exile after the revolution in 1979. Obviously the last Somoza from exile had no good to say about Carter's involvement in Nicaragua and blamed him for hastening his downfall.

Miguel de Escoto walked with me around the housing project and mentioned his plan to have a Via Crucis, as a march for peace from the war zone at Jalapa, on the border with Honduras, to Managua during Holy Week. An Easter rally would culminate the march in the Plaza of the old cathedral, standing in ruins since the 1972 earthquake.

Though I then knew nothing about Via Cruces, I was interested in participating, so a few weeks later Jim and Matt drove with a young neighbor and grade school teacher, Maria Matamoros, and me to Esteli to meet the marchers. In Sebaco Jim and Matt left Maria and me to walk with the Via Crucis for a total of eight days. I had no idea what I was getting myself into, and my thirty-five page journal of the experiences has long since been lost. However, many impressions remain vivid in my memory.

Most of the people marching were simple country folk who were very committed to this expression of their desire for peace. Their lives, and those of their youth drafted by the military, were on the line. Reports of Reagan's subversive book on how to destroy Nicaragua from within, written before his re-election, had caused much fear and terror. Overt and covert financing of the contras stacked the odds, and U.S. planes flying over Nicaraguan airspace breaking the sound barrier and the mining of harbors gave credibility to the Sandinistas' warning that the enemy was not just their blood brothers who had benefited from Somoza's regime, but the U.S. government, which wanted to maintain control.

There were rumors and horror stories of atrocities from both sides. We walked along the dusty roads where brilliant orange-red 'malinche' (flamboyant) trees bloomed, as if in protest against the harshness of the life of the people that we were coming to know. A combined worship service of the Via Crucis/rally was held in each plaza of the towns we passed along the way. Miguel de Escoto gave impassioned sermons that impressed me with his sincerity and deep desire for peace for his nation. Crowds came out to meet us as we entered each town and more followed us. Some continued to walk with us, others dropped out, but always in the towns there were loud speakers, live music, and a festive atmosphere.

Each night we stayed with 'campesinos' (country people) who invited marchers to their homes. Most were very poor homes, and they had to provide for their guests out of their food rations. One man took off the door of his house to make a bed for a couple, and gave me his hammock. He had no latrine, so I gingerly stepped to a spot vaguely indicated in his dark backyard.

In Las Calabazas, where we later had a Habitat Project, a rather large group of walkers made our way to a brick two-room house. The women stayed together in one room. I had difficulty sleeping since they all insisted that I take the only bed. The next morning as we were rinsing in a nearby irrigation ditch, an elderly woman, who was walking the entire way, took old newspapers to stuff in her shoes that had holes in them.

Besides the remorse I felt for being part of the country that was causing so much suffering, my head was aching terribly from the tropical sun. The attendants of the Red Cross ambulance that accompanied the march allowed me to rest a little while one evening on a stretcher. I remember some kids taunting me, saying, 'She thinks she is going to die from a headache.' It did seem like such a small thing compared to the suffering of others, however my legs also were swelled so I could not walk. Someone suggested I ride on the back of the platform that carried the statue of Jesus carrying the cross. From that vantage point I could see the joy in the faces of the believers of all ages, bringing armloads of flowers and palm branches to adorn the float.

A different view was seen by Pedro Xavier Solis, PAC's grandson. Solis noted in Pablo Antonio Cuadra: Itinerary that the *'Popular Church movement had their own media and full access to the powerful state media, including all of the television stations, 80% of the radio stations, and two of the three existing newspapers.'* Besides that the popular church had a whole battery of theologians who were the voice of Liberation Theology. Even with all this support, Solis noted that 'The Popular Church was not popular. He quotes the Peruvian novelist, Mario Vargas Llosa in the New York Times: *'The Popular Church is composed principally by members of the elite religious —priests and laity— whose intellectual disquisitions and social-political work is beyond the reach of Catholic poor. The efforts of the leaders of the Popular Church only encounter response among middle class intellectuals and militants.'*[5]

5.   (Solis Cuadra, Pablo Antonio Cuadra: Itinerary 1996, pp. 183-184)

Obviously, that was not my experience. I saw the faith of people shine in their eyes and expressed in their service to those of us, 'pilgrims' and in their enthusiastic welcoming of Miguel De Escoto. I only remember one negative comment from a shop owner where I was buying a snack. She said she did not go in for such public expressions and preferred to stay at home.

The last night before we neared Managua in Tipitapa, walkers loaded into the back of large transport trucks, standing room only, and taken to an auditorium where the speeches by local Sandinista leaders seemed more politically heated. People were grumbling about unfair food distribution. I felt vulnerable and fearful that night in the dark house where we were housed with many others.

The last morning all were enthused that we were coming to the end of our pilgrimage and waves of campesinos joined us —including Jim and Matt— in front of the impressive ruins of the old Cathedral in Managua. There were fourteen priests seated on the vast, spotlighted porch/entrance to the abandoned cathedral. Many speeches were made in the midst of carnival like festivities, with venders offering ice-cream, drinks, and snacks. Torches lit the plaza, and there were even some stuntmen who ran in flames through the crowd.

Though PAC described Nicaragua as a 'Processional People[6], and the Via Crucis is a yearly traditional format for processions, I did not continue my interest after that first experience until we began having Easter camps with our Vida Joven leaders. To give them a meaningful experience of repentance and expectancy before the joyous Easter sunrise service, we used several different meditations based on the fourteen stages of the Way of the Cross.

It was not until July 2007, five years after PAC's death, that I read for the first time his Via Crucis, which vividly portrays the experience of Christ on carrying His cross. Within the poetic words the reader can glimpse the meaning of that event for PAC, within the context of Nicaragua's history, of the call of Jesus for each of us to take up the cross and follow Him.

---

6.   (Cuadra P. A., El Nicaragüense, 1993; 13th edition 2004, p. 55)

Catholic theologian, Yepes Boscan, analyzing this collection of poems states: '*The context of PAC's Via Crucis is the Sandinista Revolution in process, the country laid waste by an internal war, and a Church harassed and betrayed. Traces of this atmosphere remain in various stations.*'

Cuadra, as '*gifted artist, poet, writer, when focused as a believer on the theme of the Passion and Crucifixion of the Lord, involuntarily transforms the poetic impulse into unstoppable desire in prayer that reaches the fullness of the gifts and mysteries of that prayer.*'

In the Via Crucis PAC expresses the prayer of the pain, reconciliation and penitence for '*the affronts and sins both personal and as a society of the Nicaraguan people...a petition for collective forgiveness.*' ...*In this prayer we become the Sons of God for whom all of creation longs. Romans 8:26* [7]

---

7.   (Yepes Boscan, 1996, pp. vii-ix)

WAY OF THE CROSS

Station I

JESUS IS CONDEMNED TO DEATH

Ananias condemns Jesus and it is Power that condemns Humility.
Caiafas, the High Priest, condemns Jesus as propitiatory victim,
as Lamb.
The mobs shouted: Crucify him! Because the Messiah is not
/political.
Pilate is the cowardice that washed his hands and condemned
/innocence.
The Zealots rejected him and preferred Barrabas
because Christ is not subversive.
The Pharisees accused him of being subversive.
Also we ourselves judge Jesus.
Our times judge Christ once again. What is our verdict?
Oh, Lord Jesus! With our sins we have been excessive and
we have condemned you to death;
Do not permit us, Lord, to go back to making ourselves blind, and
/that we condemn
Innocence.
Do not permit our pride to go back to sacrifice Humility
Do not permit our mind to invent an obscene judgment
in order to reject your Gospel.
That never a deceptive excuse, egotistical or political,
that never the 'reason of State', nor scientific pretentiousness,
nor class hate,
nor race hate
deceive our consciences and condemn you.
May your grace, Lord, cleanse our eyes in this time of confusion
to know you again always
in the authority of your Church
in the doctrine of your Church
in poverty, in defenselessness and in renunciation!

Station II
JESUS CARRIES THE CROSS

It is difficult for you to understand the redeeming desire with
/which Christ
takes up the cross and carries it.
It is inconceivable: the total contradiction:
Torture and Innocence.
The cruelty of man has invented the Cross,
But the love of God converts it into 'the sign of the Son of Man.'
God and suffering have been united. This sign unites them 'More.'
The Sign of the Cross.
Christ is the Word and even in his silence he is Word.
This is now the first letter in the ABC's of God.
From now on this is the integral sign of Man and his destiny.
The Cross: one God who comes down to earth and redeems man,
and one redeemed man who is able to rise to heaven.
The Cross, one God who opens his arms to all men
and some men who at last know they are brothers.
This is the sign of the Kingdom. But at what price?
With what will I pay you, Lord, that which you have given for my
/rescue?
Come, Cross, sign of the great King! May your Kingdom come to us!

Station III

JESUS FALLS UNDER THE WEIGHT OF THE CROSS

You have fallen on the earth, the earth that You created.
The God that we men imagine is the God of Power.
And the Messiah for whom our stubborn hearts wait
is the messenger of that Power.
The superiority. The magnificence.
But since Jesus carried his cross we begin to see the reverse
                              of the trauma.
The God of God, the true God of the true God
is the God who loves.
And his Messiah does not urge the death of his soldiers
but instead offers his life for his brothers.
One God whose knees bend under him, and he falls to earth.
Know in this fallen Jesus the weakness of your God
the Humility of your God!
Here is the incomprehensible and marvelous homage of God to
                                                        /man.
This is the God who washed your feet in the Upper Room.
He that falls to recognize the value of your smallness.
Christian:
It's like this: humble, on your knees, accepting your cross,
when you are like this you are greatest in God's measure.

Station IV

JESUS ENCOUNTERS HIS MOTHER

The Mother and the Son.
In the eyes of the Mother is also the gaze of the Father:
The two —heaven and earth— give up their Son.
And the Son himself gives all.
Never has been summed up so much love.
This is the Son in whom the Father has all his pleasures.
This is the Son in whom the Mother has all her pleasures.
They lose their Son so that you win him.
And the Son loses his life so that you gain it.

Oh, Jesus, my God!
Pierced by these disturbing looks,
accept me. Repentant of my offenses: receive me!
I also want to give myself, my all for You.
Only in You do I want to have all my pleasures.

Station V
SIMON OF CYRENE HELPS JESUS CARRY THE CROSS

Lord Jesus:
Your Mother has joined with your Passion.
Now, with Simon of Cyrene, our hour is come.
With our clumsiness, with our poor strengths,
                    weakened by our sins,
this is our hour to put in the shoulder and help you with the cross.
To join ourselves with you in your Passion.
We want to help you to sustain the weight of your persecuted
                                    /Church.
The weight of Power that oppresses Love.
The weight of Hate that assaults against innocence.
The weight of Injustice that you support in your poor.
It is the weight of Evil.

Lord Jesus: may this be our glory!
to take from you a little of the weight of the cross
and to carry it upon our shoulders.

Station VI
VERONICA CLEANS THE FACE OF JESUS

The man was called to help you. Now the woman comes forth,
from among the hostile mass, with audacity and feminine delicacy.
With a veil cleaned your divine face
filthy from sweat, saliva, and dust.
You reward, Lord, the love, engraving your savior countenance
for the one who helps you.
'What you do to the smallest of mankind, you do to Me.'
But here in the veil of Veronica we see with pain
                         three imprints of your face.
The imprint of ridicule, the imprint of desecration,
and the imprint of betrayal.

The imprint of ridicule —because never has been woven a more
                                   /wounding ridicule—
              left on your face
              the Crown of thorns.
Lord: never may our hands weave false crowns
to ridicule the purity of woman, the generosity of youth
              or the need of your poor!

The imprint of desecration remains on your cheek inflamed by the
                                   /blows of utmost contempt.
Oh my God! May never our hand nor our word
desecrate the face of man which is your face!
May we never, nor our children,
be induced to the dark pleasure of desecrating the Sacred!

The imprint of betrayal is less visible, but the most indelible.
It is the imprint of the kiss of Judas.

Oh, Lord Jesus Christ: this is the blow that wounds deepest:
the betrayal of a friend!
Do not allow, ever, we beg you, for love to be corrupted by
/betrayal
or that a child be scandalized
or a youth lose his faith
or the people stay orphaned from their God
by the betrayal of his disciples!
May never again be repeated, ever, about us from your lips
the reproach that you directed to Judas: 'Friend, is it for this you
/have come?'

Station VII
JESUS FALLS FOR THE SECOND TIME

In the first fall, Lord, you taught us the mystery
of a humble God.
But you fall again and in your new fall you say to us:
—The stature of man is humility.
Man has mistaken the measure of glory.
It is not Power. Nor Riches.
If God is Love, the glory of man and the splendor of humanity
is love.
Falling for the second time, oh, painful preacher! you tell us:
—This fall is called compassion!
I am here at the lowest level,
face to face with the one who sleeps on the hard ground of the
                                                        /dungeon,
of the one who is trodden underfoot, of the tortured, of the fallen
                                                        /like I am
among the ridicule and the shouts of the mob.
Like a worm, says Isaiah.
Because you have come to rescue even the last little crumb
of human misery;
Oh, Lord Jesus Christ, help me to descend the ladders
of pride and vainglory
to reach this level of your merciful and compassionate love.

Station VIII
JESUS CONSOLES THE WOMEN OF JERUSALEM

And among the multitude some women were deeply moved and
/weeping.
And He forgot his pain and his fatigue in order to say to them:
'Women of Jerusalem, do not weep for Me,
weep for yourselves and for your children...'
And he announced to Jerusalem the days of its destruction.
And he announced to Jerusalem the days of today, nations at war
nations who kill themselves and destroy themselves
nations torn apart by terror and crime and violence.
Because if hatred satiates itself like this against love,
what will be violence against violence?
If this is what they do to green firewood
what will they do to the dry?
Women of the world:
it is not weeping, but forgiveness;
it is not sterile affliction, but fertile love
that achieves peace.

Station IX

JESUS FALLS FOR THE THIRD TIME

Man asphyxiated by misery; man with no way out.
Man tortured.
Man at the limit of pain: they insist you destroy your friend
deny your faith.
Man in the agony of incurable disease.
Man persecuted, harassed, sold.
Desperate man: without Hope
this is the third fall, the ultimate
and God falls in order to be at your side: Do not give up Hope!
It is Hope in person that is at your side!
Look at him! He now does not have any strength
but keeps going to his ultimate breath in order to be with you.
He is now your Cyrene.
Do not despair.
An infinitely merciful God is at your side.
He has fallen, three times he has fallen, in order to accompany you.

Station X

JESUS IS STRIPPED OF HIS GARMENTS

We fall on our knees before the nudity of the dispossessed.
Now he has nothing, but he is naked Truth.
Pilate asked him: 'What is Truth?'
Look at him. He is the Truth.
The world was made by Him
and the world did not know him. He is the Light
and the darkness did not receive him.
Now we are able to repeat the Eucharistic words:
'This is my body that will be given for you all.'
Nothing covers him. He has been stripped of everything for you.
He has been stripped of his clothing and is going to be stripped of
/his blood.
A youth of thirty and three years is going to be sacrificed.
He is stripped of his life's work.
Not only is he condemned to death but to failure.
They snatched violently away his life, but also his honor.
He is going to die between two thieves, in an ignominious,
/disgraceful gallows.

Oh, my God and my Lord:
Once again your gaze crosses with the gaze of your Mother
and the universe is overtaken with apprehension.
The sword penetrates to the depths.
Total poverty in his birth.
Total nudity in his death.
Allow us, Jesus, by the mystery of your relinquishment,
to comprehend and fulfill your words
that we hear from your lips as Judge:
'I was hungry and you gave me to eat,
I was thirsty and you gave me drink,
I was naked and you clothed me.'

Station XI

JESUS IS NAILED TO THE CROSS

'Now you can rest' —said Jesus to his disciples in the garden.
Now it is He, only He, who receives the assault of hate,
of cruelty, of cowardice and of the power of darkness.
How much you have suffered, Lord, but the worst is still to come!
The King occupies his throne!
Your back wounded by the flagellation they have placed
upon the rough wood
and the executioner lifts the hammer.
Oh, my Redeemer, this nail that dares to venture through the joints
/of your hand
concentrates all the aberration of mankind
and all the sin of the world.
And this is the hand that raises the dead,
the hand that cures the sick.
But not enough. Again the hammer lifts itself and nails.
Why break this hand that already was worn from giving?
Why do you wound infinite generosity?
Was it not his hand that returned sight to the blind?
Was it not this hand that shared bread with the multitudes?
But it is not enough. Again the hammer exalts itself and nails.
Nails those fatigued feet because hate
wants to stop the pastor of the flock.
They have nailed your two feet. They have detained the Walker.
Have they now closed to you all roads?
Crime always believes it must exterminate its victim.
The persecutor always believes that the persecuted will be
/terminated.
Now they lift you, Lord, in an insufferable pain.
They believe they have finished with you
and they are fulfilling your word.
'When I am lifted from the earth
I will draw all to Me.'

Station XII

JESUS DIES ON THE CROSS

'It was the sixth hour,' —says Luke. The hour of the New
/Testament.
Total Poverty will give mankind the inheritance of infinite riches.
The King gives away his kingdom:
—To the soldiers who crucify him he assigns,
so that the prophecies be fulfilled: his garments. And his
/forgiveness.
—To the thief who accompanies him in the torture, Paradise.
—To the disciple who represents us at Golgotha: his Mother.
—To the Church, which is his body, he gives the inheritance
of his blood and the water from his side for forgiveness and grace.
—And again to his Church he gives his thirst.
I thirst! he said. Oh, insatiable thirst!
Oh, the missionary and saving thirst of Christ!
But for Himself alone he reserves the ultimate and most bitter drink
from his chalice:
being completely abandoned.
'Father, why have you abandoned me?'
This desolate scream is directed to the Father, but you, sinner,
listen to it.
No one has fallen so deep that they cannot hear this scream.
This scream is heard, and keeps on being heard in the heavens,
in the earth, and in hell.
This scream is the scream of your Redeemer who will be with you
when everything fails you
and when you lack everything.
This is his ultimate inheritance gift. He has cried out to heaven and
/the closed heaven
has opened for Him suddenly and for all those who believe
/in Him.

Listen: now closes his Testament:
—'Father, into your hands I commit my spirit.'
It is the supreme and ultimate revelation of the Word.
A father, a Father God, waits for you with open arms.
Because he has covered you with the skin of the Sacrifice Lamb,
and you have come close to Isaac, who touches you with blind
                                                              /love,
and blesses you, knowing you as his son.

Station XIII
JESUS IS LOWERED FROM THE CROSS AND GIVEN TO HIS MOTHER

In Bethlehem, oh Mother! you gave birth in the joy and ecstasy of
/love.
And the heavens filled with angels.
Here has been Mother in the pain and suffering.
And the heavens filled themselves with darkness.
There, Joseph of Nazareth, your husband, took the child and laid
/him
in the manger.
Here, Joseph of Arimathea gives to you your dead Son
who reclines on your breast.
Once again you have said, Trust! and you are our Co-redeemer.
Oh, Mary: in every moment of our history of salvation
you have been present!
You have been the Silence joined with the Word.
You have been the Tear together with the Blood.
The face most similar to that of Christ.
And the heart closest to his heart.
Oh, Mary: to be able to call you Mother
is to open the door of Heaven!

Station XIV

THE BODY OF JESUS IS PLACED IN THE SEPULCHER

This is the hour of solitude and grief.
Oh, sons of men —wives, mothers, orphans,
         discarded hearts that return from the cemeteries.
wipe away your tears!
this is also the hour of definitive victory!
The Lord of Life has been placed in the sepulcher.
His Mother returns, Magdalene returns, and the other Mary.
His friends and disciples return. They weep in silence.
But this is the hour in which Faith makes itself Hope.
On the third day, at dawn, the angels will remove the stone
and the Lord will announce his triumph.
It was not lowering himself from the cross but going forth out of
                                        /the sepulcher
that won his victory.
Oh, Lord Jesus: we have accompanied you in your passion:
allow us to accompany you also in your resurrection!
Lift, then, your hearts, sons of men:
'because this corruptible body has clothed himself with
                                        /incorruption,
and this mortal has clothed himself with immortality.'

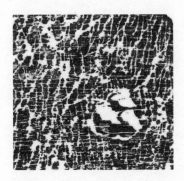

PREFACE

TO PABLO ANTONIO CUADRA'S
THE ROUND OF THE YEAR

by Sarah Hornsby

Cuadra defined his poems presented as a Religious Calendar of Nicaraguan history, common life, people —indigenous, colonizers, and mestizo, cultures, revolutions and the heroes that emerged. In 1997 PAC wrote to Guillermo Yepes Boscan, who published the poet's thoughts about the Round of the Year: '*a book organized for the living calendar of man of the Americas*' and is derived from those beautiful poetical-Christian customs of treating time, so similar —in certain aspects— to that of the Mayas.'[1]

From his orientation in Granada and the countryside at the edge of Nicaragua's Great Lake, 'beautiful Antiphons precede each poem,' describing the positions of the constellations, the flowering and fruit flourishing in each particular month, whether wet season or dry. PAC shares the everyday details a poet notices when focused on Nicaragua's earth and sky. The constellations were the same as those considered sacred by the Aztecs, Mayas and Incas.

According to Jorge Eduardo Arellano the poems for this third part of Book of Hours had the following chronological development:

'November' (written in two periods of time: 1938 and 1950) Death of the Warrior

'January' (1950, but with definitive version in 1983) The Hero and the Poet

---

1.   (Yepes Boscan, 1996, p. xii)

'February' (1950) The Fallen/Icarus

'Codex of April' (1965) Quetzalcoatl

'June' (1960, but not published until 1978) The Mestiza

'May' (Appeared in 1974) Oratory of the Four Heroes

'March' (1977-1978) The Reading of the Chronicler

'August' (1981-1982) Apologue with Elephant

'September' (1983) The Shark

'October' (1987) Spain Song

'July' (published in 1987) The Ox Driver

'December' (1984 and 1986) Our Lady of the Blue Shawl[2]

In other words, fifty years of labor went into the Round of the Year poems.

Jose Emilio Ballardes, one of the heaviest critics of PAC has grouped in two counterpoint themes the heroes described: on one hand 'January, the Harpooner' and 'February, Icarus,' as from Western and European traditions, put against 'April, Quetzalcoatl' and 'November, Sandino,' heroes of American culture.[3]

The main body poem for each month has a theme and focus having to do with cultural and historical happenings in Nicaragua in relation to the effects of aggressions and resistance to those outside influences.

May's heroes, along with November's Sandino, were Nicaraguan. January's Crocodile, March's Volcano, June's Mestiza, August's Elephant, September's Shark and October's Spain all deal with the Power of Oppressors and Invaders against nature, individuals, women, culture, history and country as experienced in Nicaragua. July paints the dream of Liberty. And true to a Book of Hours, the Round of the Year begins with praise to God the Creator for Nicaragua, and ends with praise of and identification with Mary,

---

2. (Yepes Boscan, 1996, p. x)
3. (Yepes Boscan, 1996, p. xii)

who appeared in Cuadra's Chontales in 1980, during the war, to a humble peasant sacristan.

Introduction

Psalm of the Promised Land – The poet begins the <u>Round of the Year</u> with a Psalm praising the Creation of Heavens and Earth 'for the eyes of Christ.' Echoing the beginning of the <u>Book of Hours</u>, the poet sang to the eyes of Mary, the Mother of Jesus. Weaving creation with the Nativity of Jesus, the creation of birds and trees, of waters and continents, the poet portrays events in the life of Christ to those experienced in the Americas, also God's creation. He pictures this creation of America made for the eyes of Christ, present through the centuries, conversing with the fishermen on Nicaragua's lakes.

January – The Hero and the Poet; 1950-1983; theme – Power, as the Great Caiman, Crocodile, hiding in Nicaragua's Great Lake, is threatened by the Poet/ Harpooner/ Liberator, un-named like those who accompanied Ulysses. In the notation at the end of the poem: '*Against you, Semiramis, from whose savage empire the poets fled.*'

It seems, then, that the poet attributes the absence of poets to Power, incarnate in Semiramis. Verses 18-23 refer to constellations that the poet draws with Nicaraguan stars. The Harpooner, zodiacal figure of the Hero goes, alone, to kill the monster that devours the inhabitants of the banks of the Sweet Sea.[4] Once again the image of an eye is described, but as the ominous threat of cruel Power, who makes all of life unstable for the common people. This was written while PAC was either living under the rule of the Somoza dynasty, or in exile from Nicaragua, and his writing was considered subversive.

January is dedicated to Octavio Paz, Mexican writer whose Nobel prize-winning poem "Between the Stone and the Flower" (1941, revised in 1976), describes the situation of the Mexican peasant under the greedy landlords of the day.

---

4.   (Solis, Prologo a <u>Poesia I</u>, 2003, p. 391)

February – The Fallen One; 1950; theme – From Greek mythology, Icarus, the youth who dares to fly, to escape tyranny, but falls to his death in the process; the daring, beloved youth as hero.

The month of February is dedicated to Joaquin Pasos, 1914-1947) Nicaragua poet, narrator, and essayist. Cousin and companion of Cuadra in the Movement of the Vanguard, Pasos died very young and in the splendor of his song.

March – The Reading of the Chronicler; 1977-1978; theme - Cruel, unpredictable Power is personified in the Volcano. Nicaragua's landscape of active volcanoes is background for the history chronicled by Oviedo, who described the rites of the Indians, worshipping with fear, feeding the bloody appetite of the 'horrible mouth.' From the Indian perspective, blood sacrifice was necessary to guarantee good relations between human beings and the cosmic forces.

White emphasizes that PAC was viewing this history from European, Medieval perspective, in the description of the Masaya volcano as '*Christian symbol par excellence of the diabolic.*' In Cuadra's poem, the volcano is symbol of irrational violence 'because god was mute and mindless,' a monstrosity that oppresses his people... '*the image of the giant without mind, domination by blind power.*'[5]

The poet introduces into the poetry, based on the Colonial Spanish description of pagan worship of a mindless, destructive force, the jolting image of 1970's. The poet's own children watching television see bodies in a morgue during the '*hardest years of the pre-insurrection epoch in the struggle against the Somoza dictatorship.*' He points out that violence always claims the lives of our children. The barbarous custom of human sacrifice practiced by the ancient indigenous cultures continues in other forms and must be resisted, because '*war does not make the old man new.*' The propaganda of

---

5.   (White, El Mundo Mas Que Humano en la Poesía de Pablo Antonio Cuadra: Un Estudio Ecocritico, 2002, pp. 94-95)

the revolutionaries, and model of the Sandinista insurrection was the 'New Man', Che Guevara.'[6]

The month of March is dedicated to Jorge Eduardo Arellano: Born in Granada in 1946, Arellano is art historian, historian of Nicaraguan literature, and author of almost a hundred books. He was ambassador to Chile 1997-1999 and Director of the Academia Nicaragüense de la Lengua from 2002-2011.

With homage to Gonzalo Fernandez de Oviedo: (1478–1557) a Spanish historian and writer who travelled to the Americas six times, furnishing a mass of information collected at first hand.

April – Codex of April; 1956; theme – Genealogy and Revolutions: The April poem begins, as do the Biblical Chronicles and the Gospels of Matthew and Luke, with recounting genealogy. Creatively the poet describes April as son of March, the Warrior, son of Sandino, tracing the lineage back through historical and mythological personages, both of European and the Nicaraguan/ Central American/Mexican Indian heritage.

The feminine part of April is given the honor to be traced back to *Citlalli*, the Aztec Star who birthed the father of *Quetzalcoatl*, Messianic figure, whose suffering and self-sacrifice are seen as confirming the Redemption of Jesus Christ for the Americas.[7] Quetzalcoatl 'begat' *Ehecatl*, the Wind, *'the Burning One' – in whose torch burns delight and death.'*[8] [9]

---

6. Ibid. p. 96)
7. (Elizondo, 2007, pp. 136-137)
8. (Solis, Prologo a <u>Poesia I</u>, 2003, p. 411)
9. *Quetzalcoatl* (Cardenal & Salmon, <u>Los Ovnis de Oro</u>: Golden UFO's, 1992, p. 423) 'plumed serpent or bird serpent.' Has three meanings: (1) As a deity, he appears as creator and sustains; he is the patron of the arts and culture. He is the loving god who gives life and proper thoughts to all. He is closely united to the god Ehecatl or 'word,' and is probably a variant of this deity. (2) As a king, priest, and great personage, Quetzalcoatl built the city of Tula. An actual historical figure, he had great social and cultural influence on much of Central America. His reign in Tula seems to have been from c.873 to c.895, at the latest. (3) As a literary theme, Quetzalcoatl was possibly more fictional than historic. His

Combining genealogy with creation stories, the poet, claiming he heard it from the Navigators of the Great Sea, of the Oceans bordering both East and West of Nicaragua, describes the making of those lakes. They describe the birds and the beginning of that common Nicaraguan knowledge that April is the month to burn the fields. '*said to Spring: 'Set the flowers aflame.*'

In PAC's poem 'Moment of the Foreigner in the Jungle' describes, North, South, East and West, burning in April, combine to expel the invaders from the United States, as happened in the 1930's. The poet describes the rebellion against the Somoza dictatorship in 1956, for which he was among thousands jailed, and prophetically what happened in 1979.

> *Because April lifted his wounded flowers*
> *And raised the multitude against the palace of the tyrant.*
> *The people went up waving their banners. 'Happy*
> *It was to live in that dawn...'*
> *'Liberty over death.' And the new man*
> *Will lift his forehead under the sign of the ashes.* '[10]

Could the poet here be referring to Ash Wednesday, the sign of the cross placed on the foreheads of believers in the Passion and Resurrection of Jesus as being the force that overcomes all tyranny? His wonderful essay on Ashes, among in the series on 'Man: a God in exile' further explains this connection.[11]

Steven White, translator and friend of the poet, had the advantage of actually discussing with PAC the Round of the Year, (as did Yepes Boscan) and included much of that information in his excellent The World More than Human in the Poetry of Pablo Antonio Cuadra. White concludes the analysis of April with a statement and then a long quote from the poet.

---

adventures were treated at length by Nahua poets and recorded in the manuscripts of Cuautitlan. This beautiful figure incarnates the highest achievements of ancient culture, history, and fantasy. Deeply ingrained in Toltec culture, the myth of Quetzalcoatl aided Cortes in the conquest because he was believed to be the returning incarnation of the god.

10. (Solis, Prologo a Poesia I, 2003, p. 413)
11. (Cuadra, Ensayos II;, 2003, pp. 118-119)

'....there is a tragic and pessimistic end because April, and all the great lineage of rebellion that it represents, dies murdered by traitors bullets, eternally!' When White asked Cuadra in an interview about the month most difficult to write, he responded...

April cost me a lot and achieved the most in originality and connection between the background and form as they call the classics. I had made a diagram of the poem and that background and form did not function for me. I remember this battle within myself a lot, because I, from the first moment, wanted to express April, because of the burnings that they do in summer in Nicaragua, as a 'Spring of fire.' Then, with the first rain of May, from the ashes and blackness comes forth life. This change is very impacting. It is also a symbol of the identity of the Nicaraguan. But it cost me. The resistance, in its struggle with mediocrity, lifts the quality. How many lazinesses reduce the quality of the poem and then now is too late for repentance! They say that ten good poems are necessary to erase the impression of one bad one!'[12]

The poet concludes with the warning from his, now elderly father, '*Do not look to the North when you question your destiny: look to this constellation that turns to the South of the night.*' Padre Azarías H. Pallais, mentor and like a father to PAC, repeatedly gave the same message, relevant today.[13] How many Nicaraguans today look to the United States for style, for a way out of poverty, for better education, better opportunities, for the 'good American way of life.' And the poet's warning continues unheard.

The month of April is dedicated to José Maria Valverde Pacheco: Born in Barcelona, 1926-1996, poet, essayist, literary critic, historian of ideas and translator of Spanish. ...With a clear social and political commitment, Christian and anti-Franco, he supported the popular cause in Central America (Cuba, the Sandinistas: relating to exiled Nicaraguan poets Julio Ycaza, Luis Rocha and Fernando Silva.) For political reasons (solidarity with teachers Enrique Tierno

---

12. (White S. F., El Mundo Mas Que Humano en la Poesia de Pablo Antonio Cuadra: Un Estudio Ecocritico, 2002, p. 97)
13. (Lacayo, Un Pobre de Jesus: Padre Azarias H. Pallais, 2000, p. 147)

Galván, José Luis Aranguren and Agustin Garcia Calvo who were expelled from the University of Madrid by Franco), he resigned his professorship in 1964 and went into exile.

MAY: Oratory of the Four Heroes

The poet dedicated the month of May to Carlos Martinez Rivas. Considered by many to be the greatest Nicaraguan poet since Ruben Dario —although others would contend Pablo Antonio Cuadra would better deserve that description— Rivas only published one book in his relatively long life, a staggering masterpiece called 'La insurrección solitaria,' which would translate as 'The Solitary Insurrection ' (published in 1953, republished with additions in 1973 and 82). Critics compared him to Octavio Paz and Charles Baudelaire, he won international recognition, and when he died, was given a state funeral. Just on the strength of that one book. Francisco describes him as a flaming genius, the greatest poet he ever met.[14]

May, according to Steven White, is precisely a written defense of writing, or better said, of literature, or of poetry, the one thing that matters in Nicaragua, where it sprouts forth like a perennial and indispensable part of the national identity. The poet describes the heroic actions of four heroes: Rafaela Herrera, Jose Dolores Estrada, Ruben Dario, and Augusto C. Sandino, as if they were writing in their own words their stories.[15]

Rafaela Herrera (1742-1805) was the illegitimate and only child of Lieutenant Colonel Don Jose de Herrera and a criolla or mulatto woman. From her father she learned not only how to handle weapons and the cannon, but principles of honor, faith and patriotism. Rafaela was with her father when he was assigned as Commander of the Fortress of the Immaculate Conception on the San Juan River in Nicaragua, a major target of attacks by the British. In 1762 a British force aided by Miskito Sambu filibusters raided many undefended settlements , burning and looting, and making slaves of

---

14. Out of the Woodwork by Brian Campbell on internet.
15. (White S. F., El Mundo Mas Que Humano en la Poesia de Pablo Antonio Cuadra: Un Estudio Ecocritico, 2002, p. 98)

the captured. The attacking force had two thousand men and more than fifty boats, while the soldiers at the fortress had only a hundred. At the time of the attack, Rafaela's father was on his deathbed, and she promised to defend the fortress. Though only nineteen years old, she managed to fire and kill the British commander, and at night devised a plan of throwing sheets soaked with alcohol onto branches. Set afire, the flaming branches floated into the enemy boats, which were forced to withdraw. Handling the cannons, Rafaela energized the resistance, and the British withdrew.

José Dolores Estrada Vado (1792–1869) is a Nicaraguan national hero famed for defeating a detachment of William Walker's filibuster army at Hacienda San Jacinto in 1856. Estrada was born in Nandaime, the son of Timoteo Estrada and Gertrudis Vado Lugo. He adopted a military career, and slowly rose through the ranks. On September 14, 1856, he commanded as colonel a Nicaraguan force of 120 to 160 men that repulsed a force (put at 300 men in Nicaraguan accounts) led by Walker's friend Byron Cole at Hacienda San Jacinto.

Félix Rubén García Sarmiento (1867, Metapa, Matagalpa, Nicaragua – 1916, León, Nicaragua), known as **Rubén Darío**, was a Nicaraguan poet who initiated Spanish-American literary movement known as *modernismo* (modernism) that flourished at the end of the 19th century. Darío has had a great and lasting influence on 20th-century Spanish literature and journalism. He has been praised as the "Prince of Castilian Letters" and undisputed father of the *modernismo* literary movement.

Rubén, who *'established with his radically innovative work nothing less than cultural independence of Hispano-American in relation to Spain, appears as a pirate in May.'* Darío's goal consisted of a defense of an Americanized Spanish language against its future potential destruction given the political, economic, ideological or cultural dominance exerted by the English language. White cites Darío's poem 'The Swans': *'How many millions of men will speak English.'*[16]

---

16. Ibid. p. 99

Augusto Sandino represents the other aspect of language and its interstices, those spaces that many times are more important to hide the significance of the words than reveal them. As PAC wrote in 'May,': *'The warrior is silence.'* So the one speaking in the poem is not some great General, but a teacher of children who could be future poets:

> *'The warrior has made ambush against the words that oppress, has destroyed the names that shame!'* [17]

Education becomes a sowing of seeds, literary and liberating. Against those words that oppress is found a ecological counter-discourse that fall into the furrows and ditches that always open in May to the first rains after the dry season. *'The tongue/language crosses in May/ from silence to the word.'* [18]

JUNE: The Mestiza

In June the poet unites the two cultural aspects that are manifested in his poetry: Indian and Spanish.[19] The narrator of the poem and June (the feminine, sensual and fertile personification of this month) is found *'under the downpour/sheltered in the 'marriage tree,'*[20] which in Nicaragua is another name for the brilliant orange-red flowering Malinche, Flamboyant or Poinciana tree.

The Mestiza, the woman born of the aggressive white European conqueror and the passive, sensual Indian maiden, becomes an idealized goddess, whose two long braids hanging down her back like *'two races, two nights, like two bottomless histori*es.'[21] Watching this beautiful naked woman cross the river before him, the poet fantasizes the complex dualities of those two histories while comparing her body to aspects of the landscape being birthed from her.

---

17. (Solis, Prologo a Poesia I, 2003, p. 423)
18. (White S. F., El Mundo Mas Que Humano en la Poesia de Pablo Antonio Cuadra: Un Estudio Ecocritico, 2002, p. 99)
19. Ibid. p. 100
20. (Solis, Prologo a Poesia I, 2003, p. 429)
21. (Cuadra, Poesia I, 2003, p. 432)

The Aztec goddess of fertility is combined with water, with capacity to give life and to destroy, and the poet uses this mythology in his reverie of the maiden. He imagines the rain sculpting her with the rounded shapes of the amphora and water jug, the guitar, the dome and the arch.

She needs him to cross the river, to protect her from the deadly current. From the woman breaks water when giving birth. The poet's thoughts seem to flow back and forth from Mayan myths to Greek, to Biblical, to historical battles fought over a woman, and to everyday experiences as mestizos in Nicaragua.

The prophesy of the Mayans to leave Tula and come to the sweet sea where two volcanoes, one active the other dormant, would be a place of peace for the people again focuses the poet's thoughts on the embodiment of June as Mestiza, her two breasts like the two volcanoes, sculpted by the rains of June, his seed, his children, climbing up them – mestizos from two races, two fires, two unfathomable and ancient histories.

Yepes Boscan considers that Pablo Antonio Cuadra is a privileged spokesman of the 'popular Latin American religion' capable of creating vitally new synthesis, since it is the fruit of the encounter or cultural mestizaje that he deliberately has assumed and encouraged in the modern culture of his country, and that the Church has already consecrated in the Puebla Document...The popular Catholic wisdom has a capacity of vital synthesis; in this way involve creatively the divine and the human, Christ and Mary, spirit and body, communion and institution, person and community, faith and country, intelligence and affection.'[22]

White explains that the June poem was written about the epoch of 'Christian' history, the height of colonial conquests, when subjugating and exploiting the earth could be portrayed as treating woman as an object. According to Carolyn Merchant, '*the result of the combination of technology, science, and masculinity has been exploitation, not only of the earth, but of woman as well.*'

---

22. (Yepes Boscan, 1996)

For feminine, mestiza 'June', PAC plays with ideals of the feminine, picturing Mother Earth goddesses of fertility from pagan Babylonian and Greek myths, as well as those known in Nicaragua, reflecting on comparisons and dualities, a frequent theme in his writing.[23]

JULY: The Ox Cart Driver

In July, popular Nicaraguan legend describes a Constellation in the Southern night sky that forms a magic Cart crossing the heavens, pulled by skeletons of oxen. It carries a sleeping driver, who awakes once every hundred years.

Oral tradition, which mirrors medieval tales as well as American Indian myths, focuses on this kind of popular story-telling in the communities that form Nicaragua. The poet brings these storytellers, and their trades, to life, calling them the 'Centaurs' of Ruben Dario, those who first fused the Castilian Spanish language with native Indian Nahuatl. Those chroniclers, messengers, and forgers of new languages traveled on foot or on horseback throughout the country, facilitating communication and preserving the cultural oral tradition, meeting under the stars by a bonfire to share stories to be passed on at the next stop.

White mentions that there seems to be similarity between Nicaragua of the twentieth century and their persistent oral traditions in isolated areas, and the texts of Homer that existed as oral tradition, in the context of a specific period of history.[24] PAC often made the comparison of the Great Sea of Nicaragua with the sea sailed by Ulysses, as well as with the Sea of Galilee.

The first Stanza sets the scene of specific places in Nicaragua under July's night stars.

───────────

23. (Cuadra, El Nicaragüense, 1993; 13th edition 2004, pp. 15-18) See Appendix: Sons of September
24. (White S. F., El Mundo Mas Que Humano en la Poesia de Pablo Antonio Cuadra: Un Estudio Ecocritico, 2002, p. 103)

The second Stanza speaks of the chroniclers meeting around the bonfire, heating their coffee, cowboys from Chontales, from Juigalpa, custodians of legends.

Then in italics comes the story: how it came to be that the first cart was made, out of specific wood for each piece, carving out a flower and palm covered wagon for the bride, Maria, who waits in Tola. 'And in waiting one night is like a century.'

Stanza Three is the myth that PAC writes, in italics, which brings the present into the perspective of ancient history, fact cloaked in fiction, the story of man told by the gods, of Mixcoa[25] being confronted by Quetzalcoatl, and of July and his ox driver's fate.

Stanza Four ends the tale with the storytellers, each one; relating that their story is also their dream of Liberty.

The poet dedicated the month of July to Guillermo Rothschub Tablada: *'Pure poetry from Chontales.' 'The literary creation of Guillermo Rothschub Tablada is marked by the figure of the plains of Chontales; the life of its peoples, the speech and his vision of life. The poet recuperates the forgotten of these lands; he gives them life and makes them song. In his eightieth birthday we retake his poetry and his humanity.'* (La Prensa, July 10, 2011)

AUGUST: Apologue[26] with Elephant

Recurrent themes in Round of the Year are using natural elements to describe Nicaraguan reality, historically, culturally, and ecologically as well as alluding to how power, political and military, both internal and foreign, affect the people and land of Nicaragua. In January, with the Great Caiman, and in March, with the volcano, power is depicted as forces of nature. In August, the

---

25. *Mixcoatl* – Aztec god who invented the fire drill by revolving the heavens around their axes, bringing fire to humanity. Along with this cosmic fire drill, Mixcoatl was the first to strike fire with flint. These events made Mixcoatl a god of the milky way, along with war, and the hunt. (Wikipedia)
26. *Apologue* - A moral fable, especially one having animals or inanimate objects as characters. (Word Reference)

elephant, and in September, the shark, represent political power and human might wielded destructively. Yepes Boscan adds in his Final Note: '*Against the literary symbol of the hero, is also raised the antagonistic symbols of blind and mindless Power.*'[27]

Steven White, to which this month of July is dedicated by the poet, reflects on PAC's use of forces of nature to portray abuses of power by politicians mindlessly imposing their might against the common people. PAC's writing has ecological, religious, and political undercurrents or 'counter discussions,' layering and giving depth and breadth so that the poem contains more than appears at first superficial reading.

The story of an elephant from a defunct circus being adopted by townspeople came from a real event in Comalapa, Chontales, Nicaragua. Cuadra notes that on Roman coins was engraved the symbol of an elephant, sign of Imperial power. In the poem, Cuadra uses that symbol to represent '*whatever political system that comes from outside the community, intent on imposing itself against the will of the people.*'

White notes that he interviewed the poet in 1982, soon after the poem 'August' was written. He indicates that at this point in time Cuadra was having problems with the Sandinista government, which had '*dangerously deviated from their original ideals*' toward a Cuban and Russian model of revolution, not very Nicaraguan.[28]

In the interview PAC stated: '*What we oppose is a type of state that grows like a monster. We do not want more giants, like those named Stalin, Mao or Fidel...We want our Revolution to respond to the challenge of our history with a Nicaraguan response drawn from our Nicaraguan and Hispano-American originality...*'[29]

---

27. (Yepes Boscan, 1996, p. 237)
28. (White S. F., El Mundo Mas Que Humano en la Poesia de Pablo Antonio Cuadra: Un Estudio Ecocritico, 2002, pp. 106-107)
29. Ibid. p. 107 Note in the Appendix the article Thomas Merton wrote to Pablo Antonio Cuadra regarding 'The Giants,' i.e. Russia and the United States. (SJH)

SEPTEMBER – The SHARK

The poet dedicated the month of September to Jose Emilio Balladares, author of Pablo Antonio Cuadra: la palabra y el tiempo in 1986. Yepes Boscan says that Ballardes was a harsh critic, denouncing Nicaraguan poetry.[30]

The symbol of September for Cuadra is the shark, the phenomena that resides in the Great Lake of Nicaragua, which has the capacity to live in sweet as well as salt water. Sharks came from the ocean, as did the Spanish conquers and English pirates, and more recently United States Marines and Castro, to explore and to devour. In Nicaragua September is the month when is celebrated the coming of Christopher Columbus to Cape 'Gracias a Dios' at the beginning of the Sixteenth Century, Independence Day and the day of the battle of San Jacinto, when the invader, William Walker was defeated in the Nineteenth Century.

PAC paints in seven stanzas the Great Lake with its history and peoples from the beginning of time, both those he has personally known and imagined. Even in earliest time the ominous fins of the shark threatened that promised, beautiful land.

The story is ancient, reflected in Ishmael's battle with the white whale Moby Dick, and Ulysses in his Odyssey confronted by mythic monsters, like the Celtic 'Kraken' or Cipactli, the Aztec Crocodile who refer back to the serpent, Satan of Genesis.

The story becomes more specific in the third stanza with the strange tale of the pirate John Davis burning Granada, of the sweet bride, lady Inez captured by the natives, who raised the child of that 'shark', and grew to also become a pirate. So these fierce destroyers come, go, and come back again, and by implication are not to be trusted.

Stanza four tells the story of Greytown, once attracting sailors, builders, and adventurers from many races and countries, now the jungle has reclaimed all but the vine-covered graves. William

---

30. (Yepes Boscan, 1996, p. xii)

Walker, with pale cruel eye of a shark, came to take over Nicaragua, considering the natives as fodder for the Confederacy. The poet has an imaginary conversation with Castro, picturing him cast the same 'implacable' look of lust for Nicaragua's resources.

This poem, written in 1983 during the contra war, recalls that Nicaragua is the crossroads between North and South America. The poet names the Indian groups who migrated here and names the species of migratory birds and fish which come to these waters for safety, only to find that the shark comes and goes, and comes back again.

The poem continues with naming the distinct species of fish as, for example, the Gaspar, the Shad from the South, the Sword Fish (each one with its particular form of survival)...

> *those that climb the rivers,*
> *with colors that the drowned dream of*
> *Guapotes,[31] Mogas, Mojarras,[32] Laguneros –*
> *Those that descend from salt*
> *Guabinas,[33] Sardines, Sabaletes[34]–*
> *wet birds without song!*

> *But, they are here! The velocity and the power*
> *Carcharhinus leucas – Latin of rough 'rr's'*
> *because of their sandpaper skin; five threads of teeth,*
> *elastic, untiring in aggression, and in its cold eye*

---

31. *Guapotes - Parachromis managuensis* is a cichlid native to Nicaragua in Central America: the scientific name means "from Managua" (as in Nicaragua's capital city). It is a food fish and is also found in the aquarium trade where it is variously known as: the jaguar cichlid, managuense cichlid or managua cichlid, guapote tigre, Aztec cichlid, spotted guapote and jaguar guapote. …The species is a carnivorous, highly predatory fish. (Wikipedia)
32. The mojarras are a family, Gerreidae, of fishes in the order Perciformes. Mojarras are a common prey and bait fish in many parts of the Caribbean including the South American Coast and Caribbean islands. ..Mojarra is also commonly used in Latin American countries as a name for various species of the Cichlid family including tilapia. (Wikipedia)
33. *Guabinas* - Hoplias malabaricus (wolf fish)
34. Sabaletes (Salas Estrada, 2002, p. 249) LATIN NAME: *Dorosoma chavesi*

seas of all tyrannies.
...Then they flee.
The Machaca[35] hide in the sand:
the Bagre[36] bristles. The Shad jump.
They flee...[37]

At the end of the poem, the fish, the trees, the flowers, the birds and human beings are all pilgrims that share and are mutually affected in this biotic region...[38]

The closing Biblical quote from Tobit is a hopeful, healing note. The angel instructs Tobit to glean from the monster fish the gall bladder, heart and liver, which can be used medicinally. The rest of the entrails should be thrown away.

I realized that my motive and great desire for translating PAC's Book of Hours, and especially the more difficult Round of the Year, was an imaginary dialogue with the many, many groups, work teams, brigades, mission teams who come to Nicaragua. I wanted the tourists from all around the world, especially the 'Ugly Americans,' to know another side of Nicaragua, the intimate and extensive world of Pablo Antonio Cuadra.

Don Camilo, neighbor from across the street when we lived at the Vida Joven Progresso Clubhouse, said about a visiting group, 'They have come to look at our poverty.'

There are many other attitudes that I have seen expressed by visitors to Nicaragua – first the romance period, when everything seems so different, and all the 'natives' so happy in spite of their lack of material things. Then, for many of those who stay longer, there is disillusionment, prejudices against, and even hatred, of the people and the many discomforts, a we/they attitude of superiority. I have seen this not only in North Americans, missionaries and public service workers, but also in folks from countries as diverse as Ecuador, Cuba, Canada, and Europe.

---

35. *Machaca-* (White & Simon, 2007, p. 75) LATIN NAME: *Brycon guate-malensis* (Regen)
36. *Bagre* - (Salas Estrada, 2002, p. 248) LATIN NAME: *Bagre marinus.*
37. (Solis, Prologo a Poesia I, 2003, p. 464)
38. Ibid. pp. 462-463

This theme leads directly into Cuadra's description of October as month of Nicaragua's love/hate relationship with Spain.

OCTOBER: Spain Song

The poet dedicated the month of October to Felix Grande: Spanish poet, novelist, essayist and critic. He has been awarded, among others, the 1978 National Literature Prize and the 2004 National Prize for Spanish Letters. In 2005 he was made a corresponding member of the Hispano-American Royal Academy. In 1997 he was made a corresponding member of the North American Academy of the Spanish Language. He is a member of the Cátedra de Flamencología y Estudios Folclóricos.

'While 'September' had a Nicaraguan focus, in 'October,' the poet personalizes the conflictive relationship between Hispano-America and Spain. Spain is pictured by the poet as 'the white haired grandfather' who tells the story of three generations of 'Don Gil's.'

The first Gil, a goat herder, crossed the sea to Nicaragua, chose the mountain air and an Indian woman. Surrounded by ten trusted Indians and his woman, while dying he dreams of returning to Spain with gold and pearls to a court he had never known.

The second Mr. Gil has one foot booted from Spain and the other foot is Indian, planted in a cornfield, plowing with oxen and naming the Chorotegan birds. He married a Spanish widow and died, satisfied that he had formed a community.

The third Mr. Gil rejected the pastoral life to travel to be educated in Spain. There he experienced, as did Ruben Dario and many others who have lived in exile from Nicaragua, racism and disillusionment. Returning to Nicaragua the youth is encouraged by reading Don Quixote.

Ruben Dario recounting his life experience as Nicaraguan diplomat in Spain, (Prosas profanes y otros poemas) in which surges 'the enormous complexity of the distinct cultural inheritances in Hispano-America:

Is there in my blood some drop of blood from Africa, or from Chorotegan or Nagarote Indians? It could be so, in spite of my hands of a Marquis...(If there is poetry in our America, she is in the old things, in Palenke and Utatlan, in the legendary Indian and the sensual and delicate Inca, and in the great Montezuma of the golden chair...) The Spanish grandfather with the white beard showed me a series of illustrious paintings: 'This —he told me— is the great Sir Miguel de Cervantes Saavedra, one-handed genius.'[39]

When Maeztu[40] describes Dario as the poet of the Hispanic, he says that 'Ruben was the man who forced the door, so that Americans could be found, by means of universal culture. He did two forbidden things: chose Spain and confessed his Indian blood.)

---

39. (Dario, 1977, p. 180) Some of his most memorable poems came to light in 1905, like "Salutación del optimista" and "A Roosevelt", in which he extols Hispanic traits in the face of the threat of United States imperialism. The second poem (below) was directed at then president of the United States, Theodore Roosevelt:

Eres los Estados Unidos,	*You are the United States*
eres el futuro invasor	*you are the future invader*
de la América ingenua que	*of the naive America that has*
tiene sangre indígena,	*indigenous blood*
que aún reza a Jesucristo y	*that still prays to Jesus Christ*
aún habla en español	*and that still speaks Spanish*

In 1906 he participated as secretary of the Nicaraguan delegation to the Third Pan-American Conference held in Río de Janeiro where he was inspired to write his poem "Salutación del águila", which offers a view of the United States very different to that offered in prior poems:

Bien vengas, mágica águila de	*Come, magic eagle with the great*
alas enormes y fuertes	*and strong wings*
a extender sobre el Sur tu gran	*to extend over the South your*
sombra continental,	*great continental shade,*
a traer en tus garras, anilladas	*to bring in your claws, adorned*
de rojos brillantes,	*with red bright rings,*
una palma de gloria, del color	*a palm of glory of the color of the*
de la inmensa esperanza,	*immense hope,*
y en tu pico la oliva de una vasta	*and in your beak the olive branch*
y fecunda paz.	*of a vast and fecund peace.*

This poem was criticized by several writers who did not understand Ruben's sudden change of opinion with respect to the United States' influence in Latin America.
40. (Maeztu, 1934, p. 170) Ramiro de Maeztu (Spanish journalist), May 4, 1875 Vitoria, Spain Oct. 29, 1936 Madrid Spanish journalist and sociopolitical theorist.

Cuadra, for his part, says that *'Dario refuses to consider those two factors of mestizaje as antithesis, as contradictions that cause horror and suffering, and those that unite, initiating a synthesis.'*[41] Cuadra observes that *'what is permanent in the poetry of Ruben is his mysterious obsession —with indigenous roots— in order to conceive of unity as duality.'*[42]

White notes: *what saved the Third Mr. Gil from complete disillusionment at the root of his bad experiences in Spain is his reading of 'El Quijote' by Cervantes and the recognition of the future linguistic possibilities that open themselves because of mestizaje (like Dario! Of course, and Cuadra, also!) because, evidently, libertarian counter-discourse is forged by means of the Castilian language, modified and enormously enriched by having incorporated the verbal weight of Indigenous America.*[43]

> *And he closed the book*
> *and said: Take courage, Mr. Gil!*
> *America is the third going forth of Quijote!*
> *And so was this Mr. Gil, neighbor of Leon of Nicaragua.*
> *His headstone they covered with the ash of a volcano.*
> *His face chiseled by language.*
> *And he was the father of Mr. Gil - settler of Piura*
> *Grandfather of Mr. Gil - settler of Quito*
> *Great-Grandfather of Mr. Gil -soldier of Bolivar.*[44]

NOVEMBER: The Death of the Guerrilla

The poet dedicated the month of November to Fernando Quinones, Andalusian poet and playwright, 1930-1998.

As Cuadra explained to Steven White, 'November' is not a poem dedicated to Sandino, as it seems to be, but to Miguel Angel

41. (Cuadra, <u>Aventura literaria del mestizaje y otros ensayos</u>. Obra en prosa.v 2, 1988, p. 93)
42. (Cuadra, <u>El Nicaragüense</u>, 1993; 13th edition 2004, p. 22)
43. (White S. F., <u>El Mundo Mas Que Humano en la Poesia de Pablo Antonio Cuadra: Un Estudio Ecocritico</u>, 2002, pp. 113-116)
44. (Solis, Prologo a <u>Poesia I</u>, 2003, p. 476)

Ortez, *'the brave young guerrilla warrior who inspired all of the youth during those years.'*[45] Cuadra began to write 'November' in 1938 (because of this, it is the oldest poem of the new edition of the Book of Hours), but later he abandoned it not coming back to it until 1950.

November is the month when those who have died are remembered and honored in the Catholic liturgy, families gather to put flowers on the graves. 'November' does not trust the fervor of the cry of the fallen warriors that 'fill the calendar with battles' because these dates return in a cyclical and perpetual way the sadness of the spilled blood... 'November' also deals with Truth and Beauty, but under a tragic sign.[46]

DECEMBER: Our Lady of the Blue Shawl

The Book of Hours ends as it began, with poems dedicated to Mary, and the poets' deep desire to better understand the meaning of an indigenous past when the poet directs to Mary his question in *'Exvoto to the Guadalupana'*:

> Why did you choose the Indian that we carry
> inside our eyes? Why did you seek the depth
> of this blood, the origin of this permanence?[47]

The month of December rejoices in the celebratory joy of new life, represented by the birth of Jesus to *'Our Lady of the Blue Shawl.'* Cuadra underscores the Mayan prophesy of the Virgin, a 'white creature come from heaven...her house is seven red stars.' Then immediately pictures a Nicaraguan brown Maria, barefoot upon old Sundays, leading the country people across the river of tears –

> Where do you lead us?
> Behind the footprint of the heroes,
> who have made bloody our thoughts,

45. (Solis, Prologo a Poesia I, 2003, p. 482)
46. (White S. F., El Mundo Mas Que Humano en la Poesia de Pablo Antonio Cuadra: Un Estudio Ecocritico, 2002, pp. 116-119)
47. (Solis, Prologo a Poesia I, 2003, pp. 115-116)

we have wanted to build the 'here'
– a wide, high Eden that 'here' never satisfies...
– Our memory is a place full of tears.

Mayan ruins in Tikal, where sweet girls are offered to the gods, and so many memories and thoughts crowd the poet's mind, which he attempts to express, though at risk of not being heard. *'Because poetry is a piece of poverty.'*

(I am listening to you, PAC, and trying to understand.)

Power is never far from the humble to silence, 'to put the foot on the mouth,' so in 1986 the poet, in exile in Texas, is thinking of his own future death. (We were in Nicaragua then, but did not know you, PAC.), and he lived until 2002. The poet thinks of his friends as Job's friends who did not understand. Betrayal. Vultures. And again the poet reflects on the terrible rapacious eye of Power, contrasted to the beauty of Mary's eyes at the beginning of the Book of Hours.

The eye of the leopard —tyranny, cruelty, oppression, tortures, while the whiteness of lime covers his future grave. Doubting, accusing voices crown the poet with thorns. *'And at the edge of night an Angel comes to take away the stone that covers the memory, the presence and the promise— because there is no Utopia without Resurrection.'*[48] Here the poet accuses those who would promise liberty without a faith foundation.

He continues speaking to the Lady —the Blessed Virgin Mary, that the gate that separates the 'Goodbye from the Hello is narrow— paraphrasing Jesus' words. But for continuity and security the poet grasps his earthly father's hand, who holds his grandfather's hand, and so on in a chain throughout all history, reaching Father Abraham. And this chain also connects Quetzalcoatl of the Prophesy to unite Christ the Past and Christ the Future to the Christ of now.

So goes Nicaragua in glorious procession behind that Lady, from her comes the most subtle essences of his song.

---

48. (Cuadra, Poesia I, 2003, pp. 488-489)

Who told PAC that the Lady's foot touched his bloody earth?

PAC describes his conversation with his friend, the humble sacristan Bernardo Martinez, who saw the Virgin appear beginning in 1980 in Chontales, where Cuadra grew up. So from Bernardo's account PAC writes the description of Maria — 'the face that is most like that of Christ.' And by following her throughout history, death is overcome by the sign of the Fish, symbol of Jesus Christ, Son of God, Savior.

The month of December the poet dedicated to Mother Anna Zavala, order of Saint Teresa, founder of the 'Comunidades en Camino.' She was designated to complete the first transcription of the story of Bernardo about the happenings, the apparitions of the Virgen Mary in Cuapa (1981-1983).

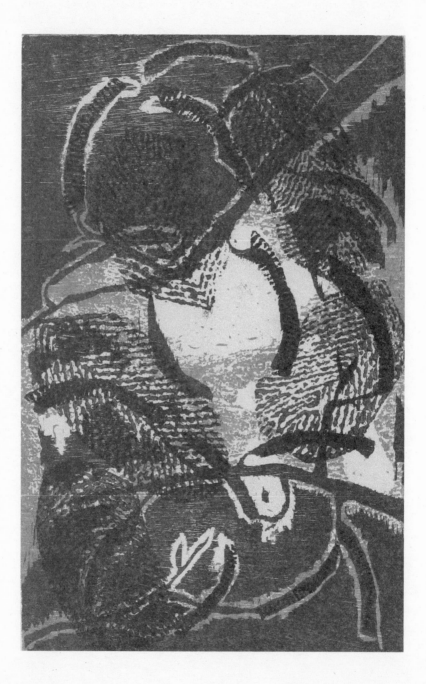

THE ROUND OF THE YEAR

To my brother Carlos, my most constant
friend and companion, who faced death,
while I closed this book, with the same
serenity and courage with which he faced life.

Introduction

PSALM OF THE PROMISED LAND

'God created man for Jesus Christ'

'In the beginning God created the Heavens and the Earth.'
And God said: - 'Let there be light' and there was light
so that the eyes of Christ could see the Heavens and the Earth.
The Father said: - Let there be firmament
so that my Son might see the stars and the planets.
Nebulous, distant galaxies, hang on the gaze of my Son.
Let the planets, then, spin around the Sun
Move like a crown of eagles
around my Son who will occupy the Earth.
And you, Moon, take charge of His dates, watch over the prayer of
/your nights.
All men may say:
we have seen the nocturnal splendor of the Moon
and through our tears we will know
that the eyes of Christ rested on this star
and that all its pale light accumulated over thousands of centuries
to illuminate the wings of the angels on Christmas night
and the profile of the friend who gave him up on the night of the
/garden.
And the Father said: Let there be birds,
so that the eyes of his Son might know the Hummingbird, like the
/flutter of a kiss
the Swallow, that learned to fly since then
to pull out the thorns from the crown on a Friday afternoon
the Dove formed with the remains of the applause of an Angel.
Because all was made by the Father for the Son.
All was made by the hand of God
for the eyes of Christ .

A tree, for example,
a Palm tree: practiced since its first palms
—since the first separation of the waters and the Continents—
to extend its leaves in a fan
and to cover the infancy and the dream of that small God in exile
when he would have to flee to the land of Egypt.
A tree, the Fig tree, for example,
learned for Him the elaboration of the fig
and when it gave no fruit at Christ's bidding
was cursed and the same winds dried with indignation its branches
/and its leaves.
A tree, for example, so the Son would ask himself:
—What does it resemble, and to what will I compare the Kingdom
/of God?
and He will answer with a smile. It resembles
a mustard seed that a man took and planted in his garden and it
/grew
and became a great tree
and the birds of heaven took shelter in its branches.
And the Father said: may the Rooster that did not know Homer
come to the Orient and sing in the dawning of my Son.
And he sang to Bethlehem with the doves, with the crickets and
/with the matutinal star.
and then we heard him obey the prophesy
and sing three times to Peter in Jerusalem on the day of iniquity.
Jesus was humble like the Word
and the Father said: The eyes of my Son will see the parade of
/pride
and the gentlemen of Rome, with their steeds will fill the imperial
/roads with ostentation.
Let there be, then, the gentle little donkey.
Let it be your mount and your symbol:
Humility will be the stature of man
to enter my kingdom!
Christ was a pilgrim like the Word
and travelling through Galilee climbed the roads to the North to
/look at the sea
and from Sidon, the port, his eyes saw the Mediterranean blue

and saw, in the same way he saw the faraway stars, the distance of
/the sea
and knew that behind that sea made by the Father for the Son
was another sea made of waters more ancient and distant
and beyond that sea he saw lands
'hidden since the beginning of Creation.'
and his missionary heart quickened and he said:
—Lift up your eyes and see those lands that are white with grain.
And it was there, by the sea that hid in its horizon the mystery of
/America,
where he touched with his finger the ear and the tongue
of he who neither spoke nor heard
and said: —'Efeta!', he said: —Open!
so that America would hear and speak
and he saw Christ in America, my land, and said:
—It also is a land of lakes like my land
I will converse tomorrow with its fishermen
I will be with the countrymen of that land.
And watching the sea, traversed the centuries
and traversed the horizons
because my land also was created by the hand of God
for the eyes of Christ.

JANUARY

THE HERO AND THE POET

to Octavio Paz

ANTIPHONY[1]

The stars of the Big Dog Constellation —that the Mangues called 'The Lame Dog' and the Nicaraguas Xonecuilli or 'twisted foot'— preside over this month: it is Ehecatl (Chiquinauat Hecat, the Nicaraguas would say in archaic Sunahuat), god of Wind, who crosses the month with his dog, lifting swells in the Great Lake and clouds of dust in streets, paths and un-ploughed lands.

The office of Ehecatl, the Wind, is to dry the waters so the land appears: the great fish —Cipactli— on whose shoulder the islands rest. And the land appears; but Cipactli —that means 'beginning'— is silence, and in the silence the heroes do not exist because they have no name.

It is the Wind that makes words: in the breezes (Ehecatotontín) that blow between the branches, in the dexterous winds that pass through the cracks, and in the great gusts that raise tempests and bend trees. It is the wind, 'yulio' of the poets.

Blackwood and oaks flower lavender in January. Coffee harvest: coffee pickers begotten by coffee pickers and those born will drink the black milk of the tree.

Pine trees in the pine forests. And early month white hairs in the cotton plantations.

---

1.   An antiphon (Greek ντίφωνον, ντί "opposite" + φωνή "voice") in Chris-
     tian music and ritual, is a "responsory" by a choir or congregation, usu-
     ally in Gregorian chant, to a psalm or other text in a religious service or
     musical work.

January

The companions of Ulysses whose names
Homer forgot, do not exist.

Beneath the vast Lake the great Caiman naps.

Supporting the islands
the torpid weight submerged in the primal mud,
sliding Northward, where the Archer
night after night lances against him his useless dart,
the great Caiman drags the dark side of the moon
the unfathomable blue!

                    ...Now they sing
the hunters crossing the rustling sand.
Rugged, not known
but already knowers of the struggle
educated by traitorous appearance –
they sustain the howling winds like canines,
they seek the hidden threat of beauty
they pry into the mist of the dawn, when the islands
that navigated in secret under the night
reunite their archipelago.

His naked feet, coarse, mark
the ancient will of the marsh gods
the jealousy of Sagittarius, whose head-stone shines in the high
                                        /cemetery,
the wisdom of the Twins, masters in the fishing of Shad,
and the famous harpoon of James, whose arm
wounded the Caiman irritating his choler.

Not in vain
the navigator knew the whore in the bustling port
and his keel touched the mire beneath the smooth waters
even before vain Ulysses put to his woman
the tale of the pigs.

Not in vain beneath the solitary mast unbranching
—like an immortal that could fathom the heart—
he flung to the abyss the questioning fishhook
that founded the science of the sea.

Not in vain
the stalking of implacable beauty
put an alert brilliance, a tense warning in its golden pupils
that the dream fills only halfway, like the crystal of the abstemious.

So we see the rustic harpooner advance in the amber of the dawn,
mistrusting, the brand held high above the pointed star
and the foam hugging his knees like the girl
who implores the soldier before parting.

'Oye!, Oye!' —sounds his conch shell and they rise to heaven
/the birds in disorder.

The hunters strike the lively canines
The dogs cry and to the stoking of their cries
the Great Caiman risks his repose
stirring up the mire
that stains the waters with filthy antiquity.

They saw then the greenish pupil
the impassible eye appear on the tremulous waves
and they fled from the submarine thunder
—prow to the coves—
the fearful weavers of nets, the foolish mortals
who cursed the daring heroes,
they, those who perish day by day
trapped by the lurking beauty
—the submissive mortals who kiss the usurping claw—
'Why (they shouted) did they choose the risk
and were determined is to remove the mysterious sign?'

Ah!
' strong men, many, before Agamemnon,
lived' ...But their names,
with the heavy earth, they covered from fear.
('Little differs, thus, buried cowardice
from hidden courage.') Who then will keep
your memory, boldness? Conquerors of chaos, who
will forge the word
that would make them conquer oblivion?

...In the unknown beaches
future girls invoke you,
poet! They dream:
If the burning exile would rise up, if his eyes
would see, from wave to wave, the blood be inscribed in the sand,
if at least in the last winds
like an echo he would hear the clamor of those heroes:
the vehement adventure,
the magnificent achievement bound to the coming voice,
he would keep in his song.

1950-1983

NOTE: In his publication this poem had this dedicatory epigraph: 'Against
you, Semiramis, from whose savage empire the poets fled.' It seems,
then, that the poet attributes the absence of poets to Power, incarnate
in Semiramis.[2] The verses 18-23 refer to constellations that the poet
draws with Nicaraguan stars. The Harpooner, zodiacal figure of the
Hero who goes, alone, to kill the monster, that devours the inhabitants
of the banks of the Sweet Sea, is the same theme, although the hero
appears demythologized, from the poem 'The Great Alligator'
from the Songs of Cifar. In the citation from Horace (QDAS IV:9.
'Vixere fortes.') from the verses 59-63 the meaning of the poem is
synthesized. Future girls keep on waiting for the poet who sings to
that first Hero: January, a liberator.
In the strophe (verses 42-46) of the canines, the poet narrates a
custom of the Great Lake of Nicaragua: they use the cry of the dog to
attract the caiman and catch him.

2.   Semiramis: For the ancient Greeks, Semiramis was the powerful legend-
      ary Assyrian queen to whom is attributed 'every stupendous work along
      the Euphrates or in Iran, including the Hanging Gardens of Babylon.'
      Possibly more than one queen bore this title. (Paraphrased from Wikipe-
      dia, SJH)

FEBRUARY

THE PRECIPITATED ONE

In memory of Joaquin Pasos

ANTIPHONY

The young month: dies short of days. Month in love and inconstant. 'Crazy February, a little of everything,' says the refrain. Warm days, cool days, calm days, windy days. Sunny days, cloudy days. Nights of stars lit by the air. Turbid nights of shivering dogs. Dry leaves and dust spin in the whirlwinds in the bends in the roads. The Great Lake irritable and changing: furious days, lazy and calm days, of low clouds.

The little Tlamachas[3] —Nahua angels— gather dew in the dawns. And the female Laurel flowers its white canopies, but rapidly its little flowers grow old, and turn the color of cinnamon. The green pine nut of the Guásimos[4] matures and falls from the tree, black and sweet, a picnic for the cattle. Caimitos[5] and Zapotes[6] give fruit. Sexual flowers from the Elequema.[7] Flowers of gold the Corteces[8].

---

3. *Tlamanchas* (White & Simon, 2007, p. 74) *Tlamanchas* are tiny angelic collaborators of the gods of the rain.'
4. *Guasimos* (Gargiullo, Magnuson, & Kimball, 2008, p. 82)   LATIN NAME: *Luehea seemannii* (guacima colorado) FAMILY: Tiliaceae OTHER NAMES: West Indian Elm.
5. *Caimitos* (Gargiullo, Magnuson, & Kimball, 2008, p. 75)   LATIN NAME:*Chrysophyllum cainito* FAMILY: Sapotaceae OTHER NAMES: caimito, sokuikuo, caimito de monte.
6. *Zapotes* (Gargiullo, Magnuson, & Kimball, 2008, p. 76) LATIN NAME: *Pouteria fossicola* (zapote, sapote, níspero) FAMILY: Sapotaceae. Or LATIN NAME: *Pouteria sapota (P. mammosa)* FAMILY: Sapotaceae. OTHER NAMES: zapote, zapote colorado, zapote mamey.
7. *Corteces* (Salas Estrada, 2002, p. 126) *Elequema*. LATIN NAME: *Erythrina berteroana,* Urb. FAMILY: Fabaceae. OTHER NAMES: Helequeme.
8. (Gargiullo, Magnuson, & Kimball, 2008, p. 30) LATIN NAME: *Tabebuia ochracea subsp. Neochrysantha* FAMILY: Bignoniaceae. OTHER NAMES: guayacan, corteza amarilla, cortez, Golden Trumpet Tree.

And the lawns in part turn reddish, in part still pale green, changing color according to the painting of the sun.

In the night —from February to September— the 'Nahua Wagon' —'The Great Bear'— with its cursed ox driver crosses the sky. And a strange witch god reveals his eyes in the constellation the ancients called 'The Twins.'

First flowering of the Cacao[9]: a tree full of stars.

---

9.   *Cacao* LATIN NAME: *Theobroma cacao* L. ...FAMILY: Sterculiaceae

FEBRUARY

to Icarus, whose ardent youth,
always igniting his limits, privileged me to
know the closest of mankind.

We saw pass the son of desire
weakened,
of floating and wheat-field hair
pursuing along the arduous hills the fleet fugitive.
Who pointed out in the valley the febrile silhouette
scraping with his beautiful shout the untouched blue?
…The envious cabins opened their doors:
'Look, —they said— youth
has lighted his torch.'

But later, when at its summit
the prudent moon began her pallid reproach
lanterns lifted, and ancient faces
exhumed from their beds
circled the bloodied fallen
on the sandy shore.

I have wept apart
hearing the ancient devotees of the cigar
proclaim the twilight:
'The afternoon is necessary' —they told themselves—
And I saw the Teachers cling in their time
fixed on your ash their used eyes, reproaching
the ephemeral flame.

What is more —the sun declining— we see on the cliff
the shy girl.

          The light, tired and terminal
returned to its matutinal virtue, gilding
the down of her naked breast and the rose
of her let tremulous and fatigued.
We saw her bend down
searching the foot for the thorn
and the town emptied the valley of words,
suspense of her trembling mother-of-pearl,
for only to dangerous innocence
was granted nakedness!

—They do not recognize —she said— the one who kissed in
                                    /flight
fluttering joy, without chaining her,
was perchance the star more enduring
than the radiance subsisting from his lip? See:
the eternal
burns hidden still
and prodigal full of beauty
she who touched his fulminating joy. Because to be
is to be frustrated.

          So said
she who was not achieved, she who remains
intact on the sinister verge of the abyss,
and no more dared the ancients murmur their judgments,
no more dared they look at your bloodied back
oh, fallen one!
where the melted wing wing still smoked its brush with the limit.

1950

> **NOTE**: Joaquin Pasos, great poet, cousin and companion of Cuadra
> in the Movement of the Vanguard, died very young and in the
> splendor of his song.

MARCH

OR THE READING
OF THE CHRONICLER

to Jorge Eduardo Arellano

ANTIPHONY

Its flower: the Carao[10], of melancholy color-all rose. Add the Oaks the lavender and the Mangos their red hearts and their yellow flowers, the 'Vainillo', and the hot wind, the hair-shirt wind of Nicaraguan Lent, the green of the fields fades, and everything begins to redress in the shuddering reddish color of the Passion-book. Red the Veraneras or Bougainvilleas. Reddish the horizons. Reds the burnings and their smoke: they form a yellowish halo that the sun turns to blood. Wild seeds and nettles gather their penances. Time makes the sign of the cross in the night: the Crossbearer (*Nauhxihuiztlan*) the Southern Cross. But a carnival of fruits contradicts the acetic time: Oranges, Grapefruits, Mandarins, Limes, Sweet Lemons, Guavas, Starfruit, Jocotes[11],[12] Mangos...

In the twilights a sun, imposing and Vulcan, forges on its anvil weapons and passions.

---

10. *Carao* (Gargiullo, Magnuson, & Kimball, 2008, p. 44) LATIN NAME: *Cassia grandis* FAMILY: Fabaceae/Caesalpinioideae. OTHER NAMES: Carao, sandal, extranjero, carulo, stinkiong toe, coral shower tree)
11. *Jocotes* (Gargiullo, Magnuson, & Kimball, 2008, p. 26) LATIN NAME: *Spondias mombin* FAMILY:Anacardiaceae (sumac or cashew family). OTHER NAMES: Jobo, Jocote, Wild Plum. OTHER NAMES: Spanish plum; red mombin; purple mombin; scarlet plum; hog plum; wild plum
12. *Jocotes* (White & Simon, 2007, p. 73) LATIN NAME: *Spondias purpurea* L. [syn. S. *cirouella* Tussac; *S. myrobalanus* L. *'Warmingia pauciflora* Engler] FAMILY:Anacardiaceae (sumac or cashew family). OTHER NAMES: Spanish plum; red mombin; purple mombin; scarlet plum; hog plum; wild plum

MARCH

homage to Gonzalo Fernandez of Oviedo
in the V Centennial of his birth

'Here where no year passes without trembling many times the earth
there is an ardentissimo and frightful mountain
called the Massaya.
That thus is named in the tongue of the Chorotegas
and it means, 'sierra', craggy mountain ridge like a saw, or
/mountain that burns.
I have seen Vulcan and climbed to the summit.
I have heard in Sicily speak to many in that Mongibel
that the ancients call Etna,
I have also heard in Greece, in the Province of Laconica
of Mount Tenaro and its dark mouth
that some thought to be the mouth of hell
and in the meridian I have also heard of the mountain
/that the Greeks
called Honocauma (in the sea) which always burns
and in Lysia burns Mount Chimera, and by day and by night the
/flame endures
and in the plain of Babylon, in the space of a yoke of land[13]
the earth burns so it seems to be a lake of fire.
And in Ethiopia, near Mount Espero
there are fields that by night seem to be full of stars.
And I know by authority of Olao Gotho
that in the Isle of Scotland there is a mountain in continual flame
in that point surrounded by the Sea of Calidonia.'
But it seems to me that none
of the so called mountains is of so much admiration
nor so notable a thing, as this one they call Massaya.'

---

13. *yoke of land* - the distance that a team of oxen can plow in a day

'The Indians had
for their god this hell
there they sacrificed Indian men and women
and children small and large
and they threw them down cliffs
in that well to the fire.'

'The summit or head of this sierra
forms a great opening in the round like a plaza
so ample that more than one hundred horsemen could joust
and so deep that a stone thrown from above is lost.
Small rocky islands and rocky cliffs cut by weight
are colored —golds and browns and blacks and other mixtures.'

'Toward the East of the plaza you see at the back a well
of liquid that boils and causes fright
a bustling or bubbling of metal that seems
to come from the depths of hell
because it heaves a wave and lifts itself up and undoes itself
with great noise like the tumble of the sea.
And at the height of the volcano, on the edge
of the horrible mouth, the Indians
had their 'teocales' or altars
and there they sacrificed and the people
left earthen pots there, and plates and bowls and pitchers
with food or pottage to feed the monster
because they thought that all their good or their evil proceeded
from the will of this god.
              And there was below, in the so called plaza
a woman very old and naked
and the Chiefs came to make 'monexico'
(which is much like counsel in their tongue) and they asked
should they make war, if the god ordered
them to submit or to die.
              And I heard the Chief of Lenderi say
that the old woman interpreted the tongue of the monster
(because the god was mute and without mind)
and she was prophetess of that hell
and he said what a good old woman she was and wrinkled

and tits down to the navel
and hairs few and lifted upward
and toothless
and fangs long and sharp like a dog
and she went out and in voice said to the chiefs
and to the elders there who took care of the sacrifices
to search for a maiden
and to cover her with flowers
and she was taken to the mouth of that furnace
and they cast her from the cliff into the well of fire
and the people stayed below singing
and crying and saying
that she who they sacrificed thus
went honored to such an ordeal.'

I closed the book of the Chronicler

(My children watched television. The painting
Of Velasquez: Vulcan
in his forge, forging the weapons of war
and suddenly the news
                    —electric, like lightening—
and on the screen a hand pulled on the morgue drawer
leaving there, among us, the cadaver:
the beautiful warrior of gray eyes
open, as though amazed
and a small
        deep
        black
hole in the middle
of her forehead.)

Now listen:

I met in Mexico the Doctor Atl and he would tell
That he saw born the volcano Paricutin.
An Indian plowed in the valley when fire sprung up from the furrow.
He tried to put it out with his sombrero and heard a rumble.
A few days later the valley no longer existed

but an irritated monster that grew vomiting choler.
Now the valley, anonymous and fertile, has history.
Now the valley has created a height and where corn grew,
grows desolation.

A volcano is the land under martial law.
A volcano is the land that seizes Power.
            (The valley were the Masaya volcano was born
            has been called The Valley of Death.)
Every pyramid rises up oppressing its base.
If you lower yourself, someone rises.
Abject submission creates giants.
Equals, friends, must disappear
so the tyrant may erect his stature.

Get away, then, from this martial month (the future is love.)
War does not make the old man new.
Get away
from civilizations opened by the sword.
—Do not turn back your gaze (the past burns.)
—Do not invoke Vulcan
who will forge in this yoke the incandescent word
—the great word which you cannot resist—
and you will give up your son to him
or your daughter
and once again the toothless old story
will repeat her ominous ballad.

1977-1978

NOTE: The text of the Chronicler Fernandez de Oviedo that
      Cuadra puts into poetic form can be found in the BOOK
      IV of the THIRD PART of his 'Natural and General
      History of the Indians.' Chapters V-X.

CODEX OF APRIL

To Jose Maria Valverde

ANTIPHONY

April is announced itself with swallows. Month of flowers and fruits. Creative and fertile month. Spring, but spring of fire. Nicaraguan Spring that bursts, like a rebellion one, with renewals, flowerings and fruits between the flames of the sun: absolute Monarch.

Green herbs under the ashes. New flowering of the Corteces, the tree of gold. Lavander the Oaks. The Corozos[14] open in their palms: immense golden flower, whose smell covers kilometers. And the Calala malaculla[15], the prettiest flower of the suburban vegetals, purple and white, botanical goldsmith that crawls in the scrubland.

April is red. In its twilights empires appear to crumble ('Suns of the red summer,' sings Dario.) Lands dry and burnings: smoke and dust. Low the waters of the Great Lake: Gaspar fishing.[16] Fish Crab fishing. Turtle or Noca eggs in the dunes. The Garrobo and the Iguana in the kitchen. The little Tisquis[17] sketches the border of the waves on the beaches. Chayules in opaque clouds.

14. *Corozos* (Gargiullo, Magnuson, & Kimball, 2008, p. 4)   LATIN NAME: *Attalea rostrata (A. butyracea, Scheelea r.)* OTHER NAMES: Palma Real, Corozo, Mamaca
15. *Passion Flower* (Gargiullo, Magnuson, & Kimball, 2008, p. 252) LATIN NAME: *Passiflora edulis* FAMILY: Passifloraceae, OTHER NAMES: Tococa, Granadilla.
16. *Gaspar Fish* (White & Simon, 2007, p. 76) The Tropical Gar LATIN NAME: Atractosteus tropicus.. idae OTHER NAMES: Gar or Garpike. '...is a ray-finned fish from Nicaragua's Gran Lago that has survived for epochs from the distant geological past. It looks like a combination of lizard and fish. It no doubt belongs to the original world of the Americas, and stories about it are from the dawn of this region's mythology, from a time when 'the first function of the imagination was to produce animal forms.' (Bachelard).
17. *Tisquis* and *Chayules* – mosquitoes SJH

182 PABLO ANTONIO CUADRA

The horizons thunder. Dry lightning. Electric nights. Only the dawn is silk: momentary freshness in which white Herons Fly.

There are no stars. Heaven is black with heat. And the refrain assures: 'Holy Week in April, winter is fertile. Holy Week in March, winter is fatal[18].'

---

18. *Winter* – Rainy season. SJH

CODEX OF APRIL

This is the lineage of April, son of March, the Warrior
son of Sandino and of Blanca, of Yali, in the Segovias
begotten by Andres Castro, son of September
begotten by Amadis, the Gentleman
begotten by Cifar, the Navigator.
And by generation of woman, April descends from Citlalli:
of the basket of flowers
—from the House of the King or House of the Star—
begotten by Topilzin,
begotten by Quetzalcoatl,
begotten by Ehecatl, the Wind,
—'the Burning One'—in whose torch
burns delight and death.

In ehecatl in chichinaztli,
said our fathers, uniting
wind and fervor. And there are witnesses
that the youth shouted, now pubescent,
in the yellow fields: 'Believe me,
a kiss desired has more flavor
than all the lips that surround me!'

The Navigators said of April:
—He built at the edge of the lakes
the scapular feathers of the 'Traveler of the East.'
And he gave its golden bouquet to the tail of the 'Golden Oriole'.
He endowed with its scarlet crest the 'Carpenter Woodpecker'
and dressed the long tails of the nocturnal 'Widow'.
His workmanship is the 'Pitangas'[19] devourer of sardines,

---

19. *Pitangas* – comon name for pelican.

the happy-beaked 'Toucan' and the 'Relojero.'[20]
His workmanship the 'Guacamayo'[21] and the 'Macaw' of the West,[22]
The 'Chocoyo,'[23] the 'Gurrión,' the 'Guis'[24] and the iridescent
'Seven-colors,' loved by the Chorotega girls.

For this they venerate his steps
and they believe him an errant king,
whose tunic of trines was dampened in the waters of the dawn.
The farmers, more attached to the fatiguing reality,
hoard for the passage of April the withered foliage
and April burned the dead grass, took the grain of fire
and said to Spring: 'Let the flowers be set alight!'

Then he put embers on the 'Laurel's' ancient brow,'[25]
ignited the 'Corozo's' perfumed candelabra,'
made the 'Cimarra'[26] and the 'Sacuanjoche's'[27] strings burst'
'Burn with your star tongue!' —he said to the crackling 'Oak,'
and we saw ignited the 'Jilinjoche's'[28] numerous pistils,'

20. Relojero: *Woodpecker.* (Internet)
21. *Guacamayo* (Garrigues & Dean, 2007, pp. 98-99) LATIN NAME: *Ara macao* OTHER NAMES: Scarlet Macaw.
22. *Macaw of the West* (Garrigues & Dean, 2007, pp. 98-99) *LATIN NAME: Ara ambiguus* OTHER NAMES: Great Green Macaw.
23. *Chocoyo* (Garrigues & Dean, 2007, p. 97) LATIN NAME: *Bolborhynchus lineola* OTHER NAMES: Barred Parakeet, Chocoyo Listado.
24. *Guis* (Garrigues & Dean, 2007, pp. 208-209) LATIN NAME: *Myiarchus tuberculifer* OTHER NAMES: Dusky-capped Flycatcher.
25. *Laurel* (Gargiullo, Magnuson, & Kimball, 2008, p. 34)LATIN NAME: *Cordia alliodora* FAMILY: Boraginaceae. OTHER NAMES: Molenito, Laurel, Onion.
26. *Cimarra* (Gargiullo, Magnuson, & Kimball, 2008, p. 145) LATIN NAME: *Hypericum costarricense* FAMILY Hypericaceae OTHER NAMES: Cimarra, cimarron.
27. *Sacuanjoche* (Gargiullo, Magnuson, & Kimball, 2008, p. 27) LATIN NAME: *Plumeria rubra* FAMILY: Apocynaceae OTHER NAMES Flor Blanca, Frangipani, Jiquiloche, Sacuanjoche, Plumeria.
28. *Jilinjoche* (Gargiullo, Magnuson, & Kimball, 2008, p. 27) LATIN NAME: Plumeria rubra FAMILY: Apocynaceae OTHER NAMES White Flower,Frangipani, Jiquiloche, Sacuanjoche, Plumeria.

the alcoholic flame of the crepuscular 'Carao'
and the 'Malinche's'[29] millenary fire.'
It was the forestal bonfire of the trine:
from his torch sprang the color of the 'Corteces'
and the 'Elequemes' and the 'Ceibos',[30]
the 'Guapinol',[31] the 'Nance',[32] and the 'Copal'[33] gave birth.

—'Behold' —said the farmers— that to us is born a youth
whose breath makes the crown of the year go around
—the multicolor wheel of time—;'
and they raised stelae of stone
with the secret signs of those Spring perfumes.

This is not the way of men who write history
—peoples who consulted the ancient manuscripts—
documented in the tradition of the elders. They said:
—When we descended from the North
by the River Wa, which passes over submerged cities;
when we sojourned to the West carried by the narrators of legends
or crossed the vast marshes of the East
transported by ocarina players in their 'Cedar' canoes;
when we came from the Southland,
from the river of obsidian that the fishermen call
'sleeping lightning;'
—there where the peoples camped – April ignited the twelve winds:

29. *Malinche* (Gargiullo, Magnuson, & Kimball, 2008, p. 118) LATIN NAME: *Delonix regia* FAMILY Fabaceae/Caesalpinioideae OTHER NAMES: Clavellina, Malinche, Framboyan, Flamboyant, Poinciana.
30. *Ceibo* (Gargiullo, Magnuson, & Kimball, 2008, p. 34) LATIN NAME: *Pseudobombax septenatum* FAMILY Bombacaceae OTHER NAMES: Ceibo Barrigon, Ceibo Verde, Silk Cottonwood Tree.
31. Guapinol (Gargiullo, Magnuson, & Kimball, 2008, p. 45) LATIN NAME: *Hymenaea courbaril* FAMILY Fabaceae/ Caesalpinioideae OTHER NAMES: Stinking Toe, resin bearing tree of Central America.
32. *Nance* (Gargiullo, Magnuson, & Kimball, 2008, p. 147) LATIN NAME: *Byrsonima crassifolia* FAMILY Malpighiaceae OTHER NAMES: Nance, Tsiki, Shoemaker's Tree, Nancito.
33. *Copal* LATIN NAME *Hymenaea verrucosa*; Amber resin used for incense by Indians of Central America.

the four greats that hear the orders of the King
and the minor winds that play to the lovers.
Ignited the North
—with its purest herons—
as a light support of pollen,
Ignited the East to transport the birds
over its intense marine indigo.
Ignited the West, the querulous
wind of scarlet, propagator of fire.
And ignited the dark South, presage of the night,
where dwell the howl and the spirit of the Jaguar, devourer of
/the moon.

Then, when the foreigners came,
they remembered Euploia, that of the husky blue,
or the Latina Hospita, Vulgivaga, whose waist
girds the myrtle and the poppy:
'Behold the mother of April' —they said, baffled
before the turbulent power.
And the delicate stranger never suspected,
come from the ocean
that the sullen witch moon would bite her mouth
inoculating violence to the name of Spring.
Because April lifted its hurtful flowers
and roused the multitude against the palace of the tyrant.
Raised the people waving their flags. 'Happiness
was to be alive in that dawn,'
when the generous youth lifted his torch
and the dried up memories of summer, lent to the conflagration,
burned. —You will not produce your fruit
if the fire does not precede you!
The flower is fire, the kiss is fire, the word is fire:
you will burn your woman, your earth and you will burn your
/history
and green herbs will be born upon the black earth.
Liberty over death. And the new man
will raise his brow under the sign of the ashes.

Later the Chronicles divide.
The Manuscript of Tula or Tola[34] speaks of April
'when he came to the edge of the divine sea
and to the border of the luminous ocean he stopped and wept'
And adds: 'He took his adornments and began to dress,
his attires of Quetzal feathers, his mask of Turquoise.
And when he was adorned, he set himself on fire:
and he burst into flames: he is thus called
The Ignited.[35] And when he burned
and when his ashes rose
the birds of handsome plumage came to contemplate him,
those that rise up, those that are seen in the heavens,
the guacamayo of red feathers, the bluebird[36], the delicate thrush
The parrots, the golden orioles and the luminous white bird.'

But I learned from my Father what the people would tell,
because the people knew of his death and my Father, now ancient,
/repeated:
—'Do not look to the North when you question your destiny:

---

34. *Tula* or *Tola* (Cardenal & Salmon, <u>Los Ovnis de Oro</u>: Golden UFO's, 1992, p. 430) 'populous town in the current state of Hidalgo. One of the most important cities in ancient Mexico, it flowered between A.D. 1000 and 1100 and was destroyed by fire and pillage in 1158 by the Chichemecas. Originally inhabited by the Otomies, it became in 980 the capital of the Toltecs and their chief Topiltzin, who had taken the name of their god Quetzalcoatl.' Toltec architecture, paintings, sculpture, poetry, and philosophy became famous throughout Mexico.

35. (Elizondo, 2007, pp. 136-137) 'Jesus redeemed the native Mexican religions of their necessity to practice human sacrifices for the good of cosmic survival that, at the same time, illuminated and gave depth to this sense of the value of sacrifice on one's self for the good of others. This sense of the ancient peoples of the saving value and of the beauty of sacrifice, of the worth of the body and blood that gives itself for the good of the world, continues offering universal Christianity a real remembrance and presence of the complete reality of the crucifixion of Jesus for our salvation.

36. *Azulejo*: Blue bird is from the gender *Sialia* (azulejos). It includes the *Sialia sialis* (azulejo oriental/Eastern bluebird), the *Sialia mexicana* (azulejo occidental/Western bluebird) and the *Sialia currucoides* (azulejo de las montañas/Mountain bluebird). (Word Reference/ Internet. SJH)

look at that constellation that moans to the South of the night.
There died April, against the hard back of time,
against the adverse wall
bullets perforated the most ancient shadow.'

1956

NOTE: Andres Castro is one of the heroes of the battle of San
Jacinto against the filibusters of William Walker, September
14, 1856.

Cifar the Navigator is an equivocal reference to the
gentleman navigator of the novel about knighthood and to
Cifar Guevara, seaman-poet of the Great Lake of Nicaragua,
who later would be protagonist of the 'Songs of Cifar' by
Cuadra, published in 1969.

'In ehecatl in chichinaztli' the following two verses translate
the stupendous Nahuatl image of the 'breath that burns.'

The diverse birds and diverse trees cited in the poem fly or
give their flowers in the air of April.

The River Wa is the Miskito name for the great River Coco
or Segovia from the Nicaraguan North. And 'The sleeping
lightning' is the River of the South, the San Juan, also called
'The Channel.'

The twelve winds are Mayan tradition and also of the
Chorotegas.

Euploia, or the Latin 'Hospita' or 'Vulgivaga': is Venus,
born of the sea.

Mirto (Myrtle), arrayed with magic virtues, the same as the
poppy.

April has been the month of revolutions in Nicaragua. In
April was the first Spanish-Indian armed clash, between
Dirianes and the troops of Gil Gonzalez Davila. In April
1954 a heroic but failed uprising against the first Somoza,
bloody and recent when he wrote the poem, offers motives
for the good part of the myth incarnated by the burning
month. Later April is assimilated, in his tragic finale, to
Quetzalcoatl; but his ultimate image is that of the Crossbearer or the Cross of the South, Southern Cross, as one
shot against the wall of the night, which evokes the death of
Sandino.

This poem was written in 1956 and in September of that year the poet Rigoberto Lopez Perez finished the dictator, Anastasio Somozo Garcia. The death of the tyrant did not produce the explosion of jubilee that the poem prophesied, instead a moment of collective terror, for throughout the Republic all those that had distinguished themselves in the opposition were put in prison, with the luxury of brutality. Among them was Cuadra.

The verse of the poem: 'The multitude rose up against the palace of the tyrant,' and the following which is a quote from Wordsworth: 'Happiness/ it was to be alive in that dawn,' was too much in favor of the assassination for the intelligence of the Security Police who investigated the assassination. For fear of an announced search, the poet's wife destroyed the poem, which the poet painstakingly reconstructed from his notes when he was released from prison.

MAY

ORATORY OF THE
FOUR HEROES

to Carlos Martinez Rivas

Antiphony

Incubating heat. Humid heat waves that giant hands wring out of nature.

The ants, cutter ants, white ants or termites grow wings and form new nests and new villages. Nuptial flights. The dazzling 'chocorrones' are the clowns of the insects.

Handsome month but maddening: full of bellicose mosquitoes. In the fields, miniscule but infinite orchestras accompany the rising of the moon. The tops of the Malinche trees ignite in blood red or orange-red. Last burst of yellow: new flowering of the Corteces. May flower. Mary's flower. Flower of Nicaragua: Sacuanjoche. Icacos[37].

The Chichitotes[38] cross the sky, red and black. The Brinquino, little black bird, miniscule and ever-jumping, begins its vertical flights, like dashes of ink. In the night the Quiebraplatas[39] and higher up the Seven Little Goats (the Pleiades),[40] that the Nahuas[41] called The Thousand Rabbits, go to seek other celestial pastures. Also Orion or the Plow finishes his job in the sky and lowers to earth. May: month of furrowing oxen.

---

37. *Icacos* (Gargiullo, Magnuson, & Kimball, 2008, p. 168) LATIN NAME: *Chrysobalanus icaco* FAMILY Chrysobalanaceae OTHER NAMES: Icaco, coco-plum.
38. *Chichitotes* (Garrigues & Dean, 2007, p. 319) LATIN NAME: *Icterus spurious* OTHER NAMES: Orchard Oriole
39. *Quiebraplatos* Loud noisemaking insect. (SJH)
40. Siete Cabritas' Seven little female goats, colloquialism for the Pleiades, or seven sisters constellation (SJH)
41. Nahuas (Cardenal & Salmon, <u>Los Ovnis de Oro</u>: Golden UFO's, 1992, p. 420) People who speak Nahuatl. Originally an Uto-Aztecan language group.

May, month of transition.

The first half of May is dust and heat, the second half heat and mud. The only two unique seasons of Nicaragua —summer and winter— struggle within this month, and their winds struggle: South and Southeasterly winds against North and Easterly ('Lestes', say the sailors of the Lake) until winter settles in, sometimes with the brutal force of the tropics: interminable downpours, floods, and the filling of rivers, brooks, and banks.

Nicaraguan literature awakens with the first showers. Reborn in poetry is the Fatherland, to the song of the harps of rain.

In this month must have been born, millennia ago, the fearsome cult to Tlaloc: god of the waters; and to Cocijo, his helper. Upon the hills they sacrificed children to him whose moans still seem to fill the hot nights like sad violins imploring rain.

MAY

In May the plows begin plowing the dry earth and finish in wet earth. May is the phase from dust to mud. The tongue crosses in May from silence to the word. The ants breed wings. The birds, bring song.

Many omens assemble in May.

The child we were thinking of
arrives with his shoes wet.

—Do not scold him.

The afternoon overtook him while learning to make a Republic:
he put a river to the North with fish
and to the South he wrote another river, with stories.
He placed a sea to the West, with fish
and to the East, again a sea, with words.

In May is the nuptial flight of the insects.
In the heat of May the tongue incubates
the new words. In May ends the reign
of yellow and begins the reign of green.
The worm becomes butterfly. The star
descends to earth and becomes insect.

—No. My country does not tire of the sea.

In May arrives my teacher, the Rain
And climbs the steps of this reduced Republic
rinsing off the clay
and sounding her tinkling bracelets.

—Let him be! Don't you see this child
is writing?
Now the rain makes him dream
and in the dream the guitar players
shake the leaves full of rain drops.

The drummers and the dancers climb the green trees.

Let us begin!
All the children
love Rafaela. When they return to school
they write on the Castle wall: RAFAELA
Rafaela is the 'maid of honor,' the freckled girl
who fires at the buccaneer. The one who shouts
beating the tiles with her foot.

My teacher, the Rain, calls Rafaela by name
—little Rafaela, why do you raise your voice?
Why do you expose yourself? Why do you toil so?

—*I fire cannons with words*
I defend names so they will not be replaced.
I fire so a child may always write:
Sebaco, Santiago, Camoapa, Momotombo[42],
/Colibries.[43]

My teacher, the Rain, observes the child.
He is not deceived. In his notebook
things become names.
Winter is history.
Thus my teacher opens his text
dramp from many tears.

---

42. *Momotombo Volcano near Granada, Nicaragua (SJH)*
43. *Colibries* (Garrigues & Dean, 2007, p. 129) LATIN NAME: *Amazilia
tzacatl* OTHER NAMES: Rufour-tailed Hummingbird, Amazilia Rabin-
rufa.

We have heard the horizons thunder.
—They seem to flee, says the teacher.
The invaders flee! And by the lightning flashes
we see their bodies hung from the trees.

My teacher calls Estrada, the man of September.
—Tell me, sir, what are you doing with that sword?

> *—This sword writes a Republic.*
> *From the mouth of the man who affirm his*
> > */spirit*
> *this sword is born. The fire of the verb ignites.*
> *This sword defends the noun.*

In May the ancient texts are covered with lavender flowers.
In May, we water our words with the weeping of the oppressed.
In May, the ants parade with green leaves
and the tiny coffins with white flowers parade in May.

With the rain, the sea passes
upright, dragging its tunic.
With the rain arrives Ruben[44] from the sea
who we called 'the foreigner' because of his journeys.

> *—I have plundered cities —he says.*
> *I have assaulted adjectives and adverbs on the*
> > */seas,*
> *I bring words for a century!*

---

44. (Solis, 2001, pp. 25-26) '...The Vanguard Movement, that in Nicaragua broke in liberating forms with a outmoded Rubenism; after Dario, Coronel is the second founder of this *'Republic of poets.'*" *'After Dario* —wrote Pablo Antonio Cuadra— *for the best formal inventions, both in verse as in prose, of Central American literature, we are indebted to Coronel Urtecho.'*

And he opened like the Gueguense[45]
his chest of gold and showed his stones and his pearls
And my teacher, the Rain, was pleased
arranging her pendants and looking in the mirror of the waters.

But in the waters of May swims a sad swan.
He has stained his wings with mud and Ruben questions him:
        —*Will so many millions of us men speak English?*
Every word is tombstone. May
again greens the silences.

In May the dead soldiers play their faraway drums
But in the camp of Sandino, at dawn,
the bugle does not sound its reville, nor does the
rooster sing. (The guerrilla is silent.)

                —*Children* —the teacher says to us:
                You must stand up!
                The guerrilla has placed an ambush
                On the words that oppress, has brought down
                The names that shame!

In May the country folk seek out, with flowers
the grave of the guerrilla.
And the heart of the child quickens, writing
in his notebook one word, Liberty?
or Death?...Do not interrupt him!
Don't you see the child is learning to write a Republic?

---

45. *Gueguense* (Cuadra, El Nicaragüense, 1993; 13th edition 2004, p. 67)
    'The Gueguense or Macho-Raton', our first work of mestizo theatre,
    anonymous, bilingual —in Nahuatl and Spanish—, with 14 musical,
    danceable parts, is the original first stone of Nicaraguan literature; a
    work born in the emotional first moment of Indio-Hispanic fusion...be-
    sides its own merits as the first primitive literary and folkloric work – we
    discover the roots or intimacies of this process of gestation, particularly
    in the development of language, in the creation of the myths and in the
    formation of Nicaraguan character...'

In May the words fall in the furrows.
In May, the verbs begin to conjugate.

NOTE: The four heroes are:

RAFAELA HERRERA. Her father, Commander of the San Juan River Castle, dead, —at only sixteen years of age, she encouraged— in 1772, the defense of the fortress against the English and an accurate cannon shot by her was decisive in the defeat of the invaders.

JOSE DOLORES ESTRADA. On September 14, 1856 he defended San Jacinto, net of vital communication for the Nicaraguans, against the filibustering forces of William Walker, defeating the attackers and exterminating them in large part in a battle that Eliseo Reclus called 'The Marathon of America.'

RUBEN DARIO. Nicaraguan cultural hero, weak as the Quetzalcoatl, but, like him, maker of culture; he opened nationality to universality and gave it a rich verbal and poetic patrimony.

AUGUST C. SANDINO. He rose up in arms in 1927 against the North American intervention in Nicaragua. He maintained a harassing guerilla war and only signed a peace treaty after the last of the Marines occupying forces had left his country. A short time later he was betrayed, detained and executed with neither legal process nor judgment, by order of General Anastasio Somoza Garcia, head of the National Guard, on the night of February 21, 1934.

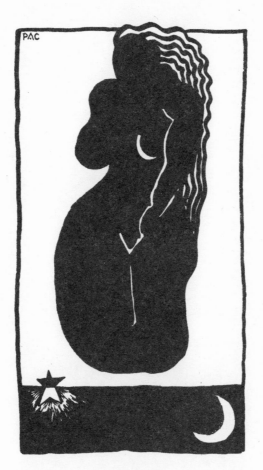

JUNE

THE MESTIZA

to Jean-Louis Felz

ANTIPHONY

Soaked earth. Verdure. It is the debut of green, the arrival of the green. In all its novelty, brilliance, splendor, fervor and power of new sap. Green in all its nuances and tones and a sinuous green that slithers in the snake, and as hysterical green that jumps to the sky in the wings of parrots and chocoyos.

Second flowering of the Cacao. Blossoms in the orange trees. Malinches that burn like russet candelabras. Fruits (all the colors of sweetness) the red flavor of the zapote[46] and of the pitahaya,[47] the brown of the nispero[48], the white of the anona[49] and guanabanas,[50] the red-green of the watermelon…Avocados, Mamones[51]…

In June, insects of May multiply, and hundreds of white and yellow butterflies fly. At night, 'cocuyos'[52] and lightning bugs, by their lanterns are revealed.

---

46. *Zapote* (Gargiullo, Magnuson, & Kimball, 2008, p. 76) LATIN NAME: *Pouteria sapota* FAMILY: Sapotaceae OTHER NAMES: Zapote, zapote colorado, zapote mamey.
47. *Pitahaya or pitaya – FAMILY: Hylocereus OTHER NAMES: Dragon Fruit, Sweet Dragon, Fire Dragon Fruit*
48. *Nispero* (Gargiullo, Magnuson, & Kimball, 2008, p. 76) LATIN NAME: *Pouteria fossicola (P. mammosa)* FAMILY: Sapotaceae OTHER NAMES: Zapote, sapote, nispero.
49. *Anona* (Gargiullo, Magnuson, & Kimball, 2008, p. 27) LATIN NAME: *Rollinia mucosa* FAMILY: Annonaceae OTHER NAMES: Anonillo, custard apple, also Pawpaw, Sugar Apple.
50. *Guanabanas* (Gargiullo, Magnuson, & Kimball, 2008, p. 209) LATIN NAME: *Annona muricata* FAMILY Annonaceae OTHER NAMES Sowar, Tsa,.
51. *Mamones* (Gargiullo, Magnuson, & Kimball, 2008, p. 74) LATIN NAME: *Nephelium lappaceum* FAMILY: Sapindaceae OHER NAMES: Chino Rambutan.
52. *cocuyos* – insects like lightning bugs

In June thousands of seeds that lay marginalized along the edges of the paths or of the cultivated fields, surge, sprout with violence, producing subversive grasses: nettles, thorns, amaranths, evergreens, vines, rattans, bur parsley, birthwort, fescues, navajuelas[53], reed grass, broom grass, brush, thistles, ox eyes, stinging nettle, scorpion tails, iguana tails, fox tails, nettles... and they grow and braid themselves and form charriales —nests of serpents, of little birds and refuges of small flowers of miraculous shapes and colors—. Corn grows and in the month's last days it is become a youthful god surrounded by vibrant wings of butterflies.

In the mornings the Great Lake is calm, mirroring. In the afternoons, almost always, strong downpours. Humid twilights of soft blues. Saint John and Saint Peter weep. With the rains, the crystal of the sky is cleansed, and the distances shorten, and the blues scale their hues from far away to far away.

Deep nocturnal skies. Mixcoatl Ohtli[54] —the Great White Serpent— the Road of Saint James of our countrymen, the Milky Way, shines refulgent. Tired, the Big Dipper ladles in the shadow: the old Nahua merchants called him Xonecuilli, and upon hiding, they would say he had lost his walking stick. Thus, June, the muddy, is no longer the month for hikers...

---

53. *Navajuelas* (Gargiullo, Magnuson, & Kimball, 2008, p. 424) LATIN NAME: *Scleria melaleuca* FAMILY: Cyperaceae OTHER NAMES: Hojuela, Sedge, also, Fescue grass.
54. *Mixcoatl Ohtli*: Mixcoatl (Nahuatl: *Mixcōhuātl*, "cloud serpent"; ...was the god of the hunt and identified with the Milky Way, the stars, and the heavens in several Mesoamerican cultures. He was the patron deity of the Otomi, the Chichimecs, and several groups that claimed descent from the Chichimecs. While Mixcoatl was part of the Aztec pantheon, his role was less important than that of Huitzilopochtli, who was their central deity. (Wikipedia)

JUNE

> '*From the lake where they fish for emerald fish*
> *from the region where rain dwells,*
> *from the site where the flowers stand tall*
> *comes our Mother, the masked goddess.*'
>
> Codex Borgia[55]

This is a month of waters.
Of soaked land. Of humid
blues. This is the month of glimmering
greens and cornfields of jade.
Dirty with mud coyotes howl.
Clean, the stars spawn in the night.
Ninth of June / Nine Atl.– Red
the bower of the Malinches.
We are under the downpour
refuged in the marriage tree
—blue drops fall and red flowers—.
The waters have made the river rise
and have broken the river mouth. —'Take me
to the other shore,' June, the Mestiza, says to me

---

55. The Codex Borgia (or Borgia Codex or Codex Yoalli Ehecatl) is a Mesoamerican ritual and divinatory manuscript. It is generally believed to
have been written before the Spanish conquest of Mexico, somewhere
within what is now today southern or western Puebla...The codex is
made of animal skins folded into 39 sheets. Each sheet is a square 27 cm
by 27 cm (11x11 inches), for a total length of nearly 11 meters (35 feet).
All but the end sheets are painted on both sides, providing 76 pages. The
codex is read from right to left. The Codex Borgia is named after the Ital-
ian Cardinal Stefano Borgia, who owned it before it was acquired by the
Vatican Library. (Wikipedia)

and I see behind her face her two braids
like two races
like two nights
like two stories unfathomable and ancient.

This is the month of verdure. Month of the weeping of Saint
/Peter.
Month of the Indian summer[56] of Saint John.
Toci,[57] the grandmother of the earth, is variable:
Her North winds bring rains with sun and the doe give birth.
Her South winds bring the silampa: weeping
of the women who take the sun to sleep.
—Look, girl, the bite of the snake
should not speak with the maiden.
Acteon[58] was made deer and was devoured by his own dogs
because he saw you naked.
The rain makes you naked.
The rain sculpts your body
and geography is born of you.
The landscape is you. The potter
surprised your body
and molded the amphora and the clay jar.
The lyre was born of your waist
and the guitar.
From your frame sprang the sonnet.
From your breasts
the dome and the arch.

---

56. *Veranillo* – month of the lesser of dry seasons that breaks up the rainy
season. (Internet)
57. *Toci*, the Mother Earth goddess in Aztec Religion, was regarded by the
Aztecs as both the mother of all creation as well as a goddess of warfare.
(Internet)
58. *Acteon*, Actaeon in Greek mythology, was a famous Theban Hero… He
fell to the fatal wrath of Artemis, but the surviving details of his trans-
gression vary: "the only certainty is in what Aktaion suffered, and what
Artemis did: the hunter became the hunted; he was transformed into a
stag, and his raging hounds, struck with a 'wolf's frenzy' tore him apart
as they would a stag. (Wikipedia)

'We made you among all others
with our dream'
—say the Toltecs.[59]
But you insist. (Have you heard in June
the loose voices of the Ceguas?)
The waters of June have breached the river mouths
and the maiden needs to cross, in the arms of the man
the fugitive and mortal current.
It is the Delta,[60] that in Greek is triangle:
—sex of the world and beginning of life—
and in Babylon is 'pu' which means both vagina and spring.
In Nahuatl Chalchiuhtlique is the goddess of the waters
—of the jade skirt—
and is the fertile goddess —of the open legs—.
In Hebrew 'nequeba' is source of water and is well and is wife.
And the dorio called 'delph' uterus and sanctuary
And it is Delphos and it is the enigma and its divining.
And the Mayans said:
'From taité (corn) was made the flesh of man
but the flesh of woman was made reedmace,
of tule —'that grows beside the rivers,
of tule —'the soft plant with which the riverbed is woven.'
I have lifted in my arms the woman of the skirt of stars
and I cross the waters with the woman of the skirt of serpents.
She has told me —'We will build the horizon;
the encounter of the heavens and the earth.'
Woman has sought in man closeness.
Man has sought in woman the distance.

---

59. *Toltecs* (Cardenal & Salmon, Los Ovnis de Oro: Golden UFO's, 1992, p. 430) *('Creatures of culture')* *The people who reached their prime between the ninth and eleventh centuries A.D. Their capital city was Tula, and they were followers of the high priest Quetzalcoatl. They were culturally descended from Teotihuacan. The later Nahua cultures hold the Toltecs in high esteem and the world 'toltecatl' was a synonym for artist. After their dispersal in the mid-eleventh century A.D., the inhabitants spread to the Central Valley, to Cholula in Puebla, and to the Yucatan.*
60. *Delta* - The triangular fourth letter of the Greek alphabet. In the system of Greek numerals it has a value of 4. (Wikipedia)

When Ninlil unites with Enlil, the rain falls.
When Demeter unites with Janson, the rain falls
When Tamagastad unites with Cipactonal[61], the rain falls.
I have lifted in my arms the weaver of dreams
and I cross the waters with the weaver of sheets.
Look at her: she invented with her blood the calendar
—the moon in her womb menstruates its phases—
She made the house.
She invented the bed and in her body Chaos was made Cosmos.

I have lifted in my arms Muta or Tacita,[62] the virgin of silence
and I cross the waters with the mother of the Word.
Mother is the mold. Is the cradle: bearing the matutinal star
and is tomb: the interment of the vesperal star.
Cipactonal is the owner of the night
but she is also the owner of the dawn.
In Egyptian 'bi' is the gallery of the mine and it is the uterus.
It is love and it is gold.
It is faithfulness and it is prostitution
—in her body Cosmos is made Chaos—.
Nine Atl / Ninth of June:
By this date the Toltecs emigrated.
The King of Tula died and the warriors were fighting over his
                                                    /daughter.
War was ignited over a woman
and a people of lovers was exiled.

—'Thou shalt populate near a sweet sea
that has in view an island with two volcanoes,'
prophesied the wise men.[63]
Also Rodrigo, in the Tajo, with the beautiful Cava on the shore,
                                                    /lost Spain.

---

61. *Ninlil, Enlil, Tamagastad, Cipactonal* —names of characters in the Nahuatl play— The Gueguense.
62. *Muta or Tacita*: Larunda is likely identical with Muta "the mute one" and
Tacita "the silent one", nymphs or minor Greek goddesses.
63. *Mayan Prophesy* believed to result in migration from Mexico and dis-
covery of Ometepe Island in the Great freshwater Sea of Nicaragua. Ometepe has two volcanoes, one active and one inactive, and the island has
always been a place of peace as was prophesied. (SJH)

We have lost countries
for women. Troy has burned.
For Helen
'elenas
elandros
elepolis'[64]

June has come from inland,
June has come from the sea.
My seed has been transported by desire.
And behold that the rain sculpts the two volcanoes
making mutiny on their breasts
like two races
like two fires
like two stories unfathomable and ancient.

1960/1978

NOTE: *Nueve Atl (*Nine Water) is the date of the beginning of the exodus of the Toltec Nahuas to Nicaragua

Nicaraguans call the Malinche: Marriage tree, because one month it gives flowers and the rest of the year husks.

'Rain with sun, doe give birth,' peasant saying.

Silampa. Rain or fine mist, cold and with wind. Is the name of one of the twelve winds.

'The snakebite should not speak with the maiden,' a country belief.

'Ceguas' Legend of women who go out at night and the man they seduce they leave to be 'played by the cegua', that is to say, pilfered of all but his skin.

'June has come from inland / June has come from the sea''' June is indigenous, June is Spanish.

---

64. *'elenas, elandros, elepolis'*: ruin of ships/ ruin of men/ ruin of cities (PAC)

JULY

THE OX DRIVER

to Guillermo Rothschuh Tablada

ANTIPHONY

The herons in white flocks emigrate over blues more intense each time. 'The Cart' —the 'Nahuatl Wagon' ('nahualli' means witch)— of the sleeping ox driver, that began to cross the sky in February, shines as never before, but the wheels are below, in the rural night, where they rattle, lurching on the stones of time. 'The Little Witches' of the constellation of Nahultlachtli (The Twins), tired, stop playing and abandon the field. (They begin their ball game in January.)

Very pure and transparent skies when there is no water. But when 'the clouds are heavy' —'you're gonna get wet,' say the sailors— the rain huddles in heavy clouds like clusters of grapes that drip moisture, the wings of the insects become unglued, and produce pains in the joints.

In the mornings, the kingdom of the butterflies is extended: whites, reds, yellows, blues, blacks, golden. And by night, Quiebraplatas and Crickets and infinite concerts of insects. Morning mosquitoes. Miniscule flies that spin around fruit and dogs. Bellicose mosquitoes sound their bugles and attack with the evening. Ants cross in crazy lanes the sands of the Lake; the 'Bravas,' fierce warriors, transport their yellow eggs.

Downpours at any hour. Sometimes even three or four chain of their waters together and when they cease, the clouds of 'Chayules' burst.

July is a month of fulgent beauty in nature; mud under the vegetation. Splendid greens and reds. Pitahayas. Malinches. Zenzontles[65] breeding. Chichitotes…But a cruel month: there is no

---

65. *Zenzontles-* (Gargiullo, Magnuson, & Kimball, 2008) LATIN NAME: *Turdus plebejus* OTHER NAMES: Mockingbirds, Mountain Robin, Sensontle Montanas.

insect that does not make appointment in the humid air of July. And the Great Lake dirty, worked up, groaning in its squalls.

Good rain or bad rain/ by Saint James, (we will eat) 'yoltamal'[66].

---

66. *Yoltamal* – Tamal made from sweet corn and is a light yellow-whitish color, filled with sugar and cheese, then steamed in the corn husks.

JULY

> '*Choose between love and science;*
> *there is no other choice.*'
>
> Unamuno

I

In the sky of July nocturnal bees craft
constellations.
In the highest silence words
are stars, (submerged
in the dream, lovers pass by)
they are birds
they are tears, (stuck
in the mud, the generals kill)
and the crow
caws at the sinister.
                              In the sky
of July, the ox driver crosses in his cart
the rural darkness.
A humid moon illuminates at times
his dead oxen
and you can hear the knock of the wheels on invisible rocks
and the grumbling sound of their axles
wasted by time.
(The dog howls,
the nervous horses throw back their ears.)
Centuries spent wandering
—from path to path—
dreaming himself immortal but sleeping.

Now crosses the falcon from Segovian nights
crosses the forests of the East
—obscured Chorotegas weave their green-black branches
with the humid ferns of the obscured Mayas—
crosses the mountains of Oluma and the sacred
valley of Cuapa; crosses Mancotal;
Somoto, the summit of Kilambe,
The plains of Acoyapa, Matiguas and its mountains;
crosses the island, of the two volcanoes girded by the sweet waves,
my beautiful white city (now lost)
and the city of Dario and the dark
native river of the South and the places
of the Gueguense: Diriomos
                       Dirianes
                       Niquinohomos
All have heard
of the wheels of time that never stops
cross the night the dream that stops time.

II

In the night of July the campers get together. Look at them! Seated
on their saddle cloths around the word. They heat coffee on the fire.
Lightning bugs with shrill elytra chirp. Mosquitoes buzz and the
young colts shake their long manes. Get down! Greet the riders!
They are sons of Chontales. This is Villagra, peasant from Acoyapa, weaver of cruppers and halter headstalls, who has also woven the magnificent sagas of our origins. This other is Astorga, the
warrior of September, by whose deeds your children are now free.
This other is Juan Rejano, the singer of Teustepe And this other, call
him Gaitan, the Juigalpan: steward of your legends. They are those
that Ruben called Centaurs. They spoke of July, the ox driver. They
heard in the forest with no paths the deaf roll of the Nahuatl wagon.
They tell his story:

It was in the first days, when the first cattle moaned and the Indian
was astonished by the bull and by gunpowder. July, the settler;
the Alderman of Granada, he who came down from the ship with

the seventy founders, now builds with his Indians the wagon of his weddings. Maria awaits the announced procession in Tola. The flowered wagon. The gentlemen. The singers and gallants who will open way from the port of the Sweet Sea to the village of the Toltecs. Master carpenters carve with adze the pieces of the wagon (the first wagon). Curious apprentices attentively watch the wise blow of the tools. They carve the cart pole in the white and hard wood of Chaperno.[67] They carve the wheels —that astound chiefs and vassals— from the trunk of the robust Jenisero[68] and the axles from Nispero, the tree with the heart of iron. Only the yoke is light, carved in the light Guasimo.[69]

Now the powerful oxen lower the cervix to the yoke. Still not docile, they pull the wagon and go and come among the mockery of the peasants. Now they dress it with awnings. Now they adorn the furnishing with palms and flowers. And the train departs among shouts. The horsemen, the singers and gallants. They leave singing. These are natural hours to depart.

They will climb the slope of the Fountain. They will cross the high and fertile valley of Cana de Castilla. Lands of bread for the taking. They will climb the skirts of Mombacho. Lands of Magpies and Toucans; Indian lands. They will sleep in Nandaime. They will unsaddle the young horses. They will unyoke the oxen. They

---

67. *Chaperno* – LATIN NAME: Lonchocarpus violaceus; FAMILY: Faboide- ae / Leguminosae / Papilionaceae, OTHER NAMES: Lilac Tree, Dotted Lancepod, Chaperno.

68. *Jenisero* - (White & Simon, 2007, p. 79) LATIN NAME: *Albizia sa- man (Jacq.)* F. Muell. [syn. *Mimosa saman* Jacq.; *Pithecellobium sa- man* (Jacq.) Benth; *Samanea saman (*Jacq.) Merr.; *A. nicoyana* Britton & Rose] ; FAMILY: Mimosaceae (prev. Leguminosae), OTHER NAMES: Rain Tree, Monkeypod, *Genizaro*.

69. *Guasimo* – LATIN NAME: *Guazuma ulmifolia* FAMILY: Sterculiaceae OTHER NAMES: lmleaf guazuma; ba cedar (Cayman); bastard cedar (Belize, Jamaica, Panama, Puerto Rico); bastard-cedar (Jamaica, Pana- ma, Trinidad); bay cedar, bay-cedar, box cedar (Belize); caulote (Belize); cork bottom wood (Belize); gunstak (Lesser Antilles); pigeon-wood (To- bago); pixoy (Belize); pricklenut (Mexico); West Indian elm (Jamaica, Panama, Puerto Rico, Trinidad); West-Indian elm (Puerto Rico); wild bay cedar (Belize).

will light the camp fire and the guitars will mince the moon with
fireflies. In Tola, Maria waits. And in the waiting one night is like
a century.

III

Then the gods came together. They sat
in the third heaven where words still
know the rude clash of polemics.
The roosters did not yet sing, the first roosters
and the gods spoke.
Mixcoa, the god of roads and of merchants
spoke and said these winged words:
—Since those conflictive men went out from our hands
they have traversed their story
on the open roads on foot: with quick
            steps. They were walking feet,
good walking feet, walking pilgrims,
untiring feet
of warriors, laborers, merchants, commoners.
Indian lines of migration and exile.
The ancient story is woven with paths of feet
            that advance
with barefoot trails, of silent
steps that leave your memory
and seal the kingdom of men.
(And the grim god lifted his voice):
—But the foreigners arrive, curse them!
And bring to earth the dangerous stars
that turn in the night.

No longer will it be man who drags his story
but the mute machine. No longer the foot
nor the vigor of the walker
nor the glory of the body but the cold
wheel of the moon, stranger to the earth,
and the hurry and the throng will unhinge life
and the world will turn in the hands of crazy and fast gods
And saying this Mixcoa lifted his deadly lance.

—Stop your anger! —shouted Quetzalcoatl, the god friend
he who unfolds his fate
between the morning star and that of the sweet evening whistle:
—Do not impose limits on man!
he said with ancient and calm voice
—Remember that in the dominion of the waters
man was not fish.
but invented the canoe
That in the dominion of the earth
man was not jaguar
but extended with the lance the power of his claw;
That in the dominion of the wind he was not eagle
but hunted the birds with the flight of his arrow.
And the gods argued.
And spoke lachrymose Cocijo,
of the moss hair —god of the rain —and said:
— 'Man wears down all and holds it down
He oppresses the sea, he helps himself to the winds
He tears out the bowels of the earth,
and, it horrifies me to refer to it,
the burning ray he harnesses at will.'
No sooner had Cocijo gone silent than Mixcoa threw up his
                                        /choleric shout:
—Men will not become as gods!
And he hurled against July his obsidian and cursed him:
—The ox driver will never awaken!'
—He will awaken each century —interceded the benevolent
god of the Toltecs
and imposed his ancient and reposed voice:
—The dream will awaken the dreamer
He will awaken in search of the face of the mother
in the face of the daughter
and the face of yesterday in the future.
His illusion will awaken the disillusion.
Oppression will awaken his liberty.

IV

This the horsemen narrated around the fire under the humid
moon of July. Those Ruben called Centaurs.
Thus was explained by the tellers of legends
the mystery of this sign.
It so happened that the month rose up to show his fate
—not on his feet, but on untold wheel—
And in his stone we saw that its date was a story,
      but also a dream.
And Juan Rejano said: —Liberty is dream.
And Astorga: —The dream is liberty.
And Gaitan, the old, raised his hand and said:
—Do not put doors on the fable. Man
is not enclosed by time / but fits in a moment.

POAS, COSTA RICA 1979 / AUSTIN, TEXAS 1986

NOTE: The 'Wagon' or the Nahua Cart' ('nahualli' means magical or bewitched) is the constellation of Big Bear and is a Nicaraguan legend: The legend of the damned wagon and its ox driver, July, who awakens every century.

Cuadra links the curse of the ox driver —who was to marry in Tola (a town in the South)— inaugurating the transport in wagons and carts in the first years of the Conquest, with the legend of the bride of Tola, the woman who stays waiting, with veil and orange blossoms, for the groom who never comes.

The wagon pulled by dead oxen is heard crossing the roads and streets in all of Nicaragua.

But the ox driver awakens every century and every awakening is a new legend that the people invent and is the image of his destiny.

The poem in his SONG III about the curse of the gods parodies the sacred Baroque of the XVIII Century, and incorporates, to give it the flavor of the period, a stanza of Brother Matias of Cordoba's 'The attempt of the lion and the success of his enterprise.'

AUGUST

APOLOGUE WITH ELEPHANT

to Steven White

ANTIPHONY

Look to the South: these are the last nights of the luminous Crossbeam, Nahui Nauhxihuiztlan: the four turquoises, the four blue stones of the Southern Cross. This is 'the brooch of the mantle of Our Lady.'

Suddenly the heat enters amidst the humidity like a divinity that returns disguised and vengeful. August with its dogs: The Dog Star. Sometimes the god enters irritated producing cyclones or great squalls. The turtles poke out their startled heads in the waters of the Great Lake. The coasts and beaches, muddied and dirty. Arrow grasses.

The mosquitos are emboldened: they appropriate the crepuscules.

The quiebraplatas in the pastures or in the plains seem like motley meetings of stars.

Nancites, jocotes of the season, dragon fruit, watermelons, cantaloupes, mangos, flowers in the *achiote tree,*[70] the malinche tree reaches the fullness of red.

'Rainbow in the West/ loose the plow and come.' (The sailors change the refrain and give counsel, 'tie up your boat and come.')

---

70. A*chiotes* – (Gargiullo, Magnuson, & Kimball, 2008, p. 164) LATIN NAME: *Bixa orellana* FAMILY Bixaceae OTHER NAMES: Kacha, Anatto

AUGUST

'Elephas Aeternitas Auggusti'
—Inscription of a coin of Phillip, Emperor

'There where reason accommodates monsters.'

Robert Juarroz

Through the holes of the tent
we saw the Ringmaster spread out
with face still floured and his big clown-red mouth,
poisoned by the Tamer (they said):
the old struggle between Power and Satire
dignified later by an aura of legend
when galloping the village streets crossed
the white horse
and was lost in the night
carrying, standing on its silver saddle,
the freckled Amazon of the opalescent hair.

Dissolved was the Great Augustus Circus.
Disappeared were the trapeze artists, the dwarfs, and the jugglers.
The tightrope dogs, wise with hunger,
sought out the houses of the rich
and in the abandoned coffers, the suits of luminous splendor
became rags with sequins of fatuous brilliance.
Only the elephant remained.

The village made him their own.
Loved his orphan form, without origin,
that made commonplace the exotic.
There where he passed with his heavy slow step,

he created an unusual landscape.
The old Indians, seated under the almond trees,
scrutinized, in suspense, indications of the deity
that time will dethrone. And they feared
the hazardous friendship of his power.
The elephant extended them his trunk from a remote age
wiggling at its extremity a finger, anachronistic and deformed
as though smell and touch belonged
to a kingdom still undivided.

In the nights of routine silences
the students and the lovers saw him move
like an obscure encyclopedia
of rugose skin and indecipherable text.
His small eyes are sad,
prisonerly sad under his enormous curved forehead
as though some boulder or an ancient
tree could unlock the secret eyelid of the inanimate.

We began, then, to invent our memories.
We began to notice that our houses reduced his stature,
that our trees degraded the elevation of their desires,
that a domain was growing
that the uncontrollable fascination of the gigantic was growing.

What can a village of rustic musas[71]
and provincial disputes do
when through their nights with his white fangs
goes the corpulence of Order
with the lunar seal of encrusted feet
and the cloak of his skin, the ominous
cloak of an unfathomable past like tedium?

The poets asked: Is he lucid
or is he blind, this power that exceeds our forms?
Because time passed, heavy, dense, and pachydermatous.

---

71. musas - poetic muse, or musa -Latin for plantain or banana tree

And his weight was a weapon. And his size a kingdom.
And he begged like every king.
He extended his trunk imposing
the demolishing tribute to his enormity.
The sowers said: 'He tramples our cornfields'
The sutlers of the market: 'He destroys our market-stands'
And the parish priest opened the Book
to where Eleazer, son of Saura —the Maccabean—
brought down the Mammoth of Syria with an axe
and he perished, crushed by its mass.

And it was too late!

The full moon
wounded his sex with the savage edge of its sickle. His love was
his fury. He smelled in the wind toward the Orient
—where the sea roared— the unreachable female
and he charged us
trumpeting his rut.

With shouts
with stones
with torches
the multitude cast him from the town
to the miry wasteland.

His death cost lives.
Like long ago applauses
it raised flutters and shrieks
from diviner birds.

And we saw him sink under his own weight
muddied archaic sun
deformed
and foreign.

1981-82

228 PABLO ANTONIO CUADRA

NOTE: 'They told me the anecdote of the elephant from a circus that disbanded because of a crime many years ago in Comalapa, Chontales,' tells Cuadra.

August is the month dedicated to the Emperor Augustus. And the elephant, as a heavy and fearful weapon —forming the destructive elephant corps— was associated with the idea of Power: So Phillip minted coins with an elephant and the inscription —'*Aeternitas Auggustus, Aeternitas Imper.*'

SEPTEMBER

THE SHARK

To Jose Emilio Balladares

ANTIPHONY

Christopher Columbus came to 'Cabo Gracias a Dios'[72] on September 12, 1502 after eighty-eight days of frightening storms. There, the climate changed, and the winds and currents turned favorable.

'This is a month of clouds like Cyclops[73]
that carry rains in their immense
black amphorae.'

Sharks[74] in the mouths of the river. Shad.

September: Patriot month. Day 15, the Independence. Day 14, the costly confirmation of that Independence, by the National War to expel Walker and his filibusters: the victory of San Jacinto.

In the nights the Wagon (the Bear) with its Ox Driver can no longer be seen, but Malinalli[75] —the bundle of grass— begins to shine (Cassiopeia). And Xochil (the Flower) that is the constellation of Andromeda: her brilliance reminds us of her fable: Cassiopeia, her mother, says that Andromeda is the most beautiful of the Nereides, the sea nymphs. This irritates Neptune, who sends a flood and then a marine monster to destroy her Ethiopian land. Fearful Cepheus,

---

72. Cape Thanks to God
73. *Cyclops* - in Greek mythology and later Roman mythology, was a member of a primordial race of giants, each with a single eye in the middle of his forehead. (Wikipedia)
74. *Sharks* - (Salas Estrada, 2002, pág. 250) LATIN NAME: *Charcharhinus leucas, 'Can be found in the Great Lake and principle rivers of the Atlantic Coast of Nicaragua.'*
75. *Malinalli* – From Aztec Astrology, one of the signs in the stars. The protector of day Malinalli (Grass) is Patecatl. This day signifies tenacity, rejuvenation, that which cannot be uprooted forever. (Internet)

her father, chains her to give her to the monster. But Perseus —
killer of the Medusa and rider of Pegasus— saves Andromeda and
marries her. Liberty in Nicaragua has been faithful to this myth.

September

Nicaraguans called the Great Lake:
'Cocibolca' —Coatl-pol-can, place of the great Serpent—,
and the Spanish, upon Christianizing the region, gave to its
main ports the names of Saints who overcame
the dragon: Saint Michael, Saint George, and the Virgin.

Alexander Dávila Bolaños

Those of the Mangue language believed that the Night,
still a maiden, tripped while carrying
the amphora of the moon. And she spilled these pale, sweet waters
where the child that I was
peers through my eyes
and reads tirelessly the archaic hymn
of the waves —in the Beginning
was the verse— waves: stanzas
for unpublished languages, rhythms
that shaped, like a shell
the labyrinth of the ear.
A child returns to the womb. Recovers infancy
to the air wept by fishes: watery birds
without song
and feather hardened by purest cruelty.
Here death has laid its incessant silence
from the beginning. Here
the sinister fin —by the blade of the moon—
scrapes the smooth surface of the Genesis.

1

I remember an old fisherman
carpenter of the riverside, working in the cove.
Hammers with the mallet and the chisel on the tow
Smiles hearing the happy laughter of the boy
who jumps among the waves
And all as always. 'About pain
the ancient teachers were never wrong.'[76]

Pitch bubbling in the pot on the brazier.
The sailboat and its dissipated
voices nearing the port. The whisper
of the wind. And the scream. And the heron
immobile on the branch.
Where the devil has this boy gone?

2

It was in the month of September
And 'I, Ishmael, formed part of that crew.'
The fisherman came down from the islands
and traced the water with lamps.

Ancient waters
where the signs are erased. Black
waters, antecedent to the moon, where passes
like blame, in the depths, the ominous
shadow.

Were not the giants
already overcome? —murmurs the mariner.
Did not Cuajipal[77] —son of the mire—

---

76. *W.H. Auden – 'Palais des Beaux Arts.'*
77. *Cuajipal*–LATIN NAME: *Caiman crocodilus fuscus* OTHER NAMES:
     OTHER NAMES: Brown Caiman, American Caiman, Cuajipal, Dusky
     caiman, Jacaretinga, Lagarto Chato, Lagarto de Concha, Lagarto negro,
     Magdalena caiman, Pululo, Talulín, Wizizil. (Internet)

he who supports on his back the weight of the islands
fall under the sharp harpoon of January?
—It is Scylla[78] —said the foreigner,
she who saw Odysseus and howls
on the black waves beaten by the Trade Winds.
Others said: —The Kraken![79] the deceiver!
on whose back —believing it an island—
the priests of the Most High celebrated Mass.
—Or Cipactli[80] —said the old man,
remembering the dreadful newcomer, son of the sea,
and lifted his lamp
illuminating the rocks of the cliff

---

78. *Scylla* - According to Ovid, Scylla was once a beautiful nymph. The fisherman-turned-sea-god Glaucus fell madly in love with her, but she fled from him onto the land where he could not follow. Despair filled his heart. He went to the sorceress Circe...who prepared a vial of very powerful poison and poured it in the pool where Scylla bathed. As soon as the nymph entered the water, she was transformed into a frightful monster with twelve feet and six heads, each with three rows of teeth. Angry, growling wolf heads grew from her waist, and she tried to brush them off. She stood there in utter misery, unable to move, loathing and destroying everything that came into her reach, a peril to all sailors who passed near her. Whenever a ship passed, each of her heads would seize one of the crew. Scylla is rationalised in the *Aeneid* as a dangerous rock outcropping.... In Homer's *Odyssey* XII, Odysseus is given advice by Circe to sail closer to Scylla, for Charybdis could drown his whole ship: "Hug Scylla's crag—sail on past her—top speed! Better by far to lose six men and keep your ship than lose your entire crew" she warns... Odysseus then successfully sails his ship past Scylla and Charybdis, but Scylla manages to catch six of his men, devouring them alive...(Wikipedia)

79. *Kraken* - legendary sea monsters of gargantuan size, said to have dwelt off the coasts of Norway and Iceland. The sheer size and fearsome appearance attributed to the beasts...have originated from sightings of real giant squid that are variously estimated to grow to 13–15 m (40–50 ft) in length, including the tentacles... (Wikipedia)

80. *Cipactli* - In Aztec mythology, Cipactli was a vicious monster, part crocodile and part fish. (Wikipedia)

where an Indian hand engraved centuries ago
his stony chronicle:...the same story!
Five dentate circles and in the center
the face of a boy!
Because it is ancient
                    and immutable.

It goes out to sea
and returns. It crosses
the impenetrable liquids millions from the Devonic age[81]
—swims in Genesis—
and comes back
—always the same— and always
you hear sculpted in the wind or in the rock
the scream!

3

In the handsome cavity excavated with your claws
—cave of your dreams— where you frolic in your tawny evenings
old god of water, here, from shore to shore
—between the barren mast that gives breath to the adventure
and the flowered tree where order rests—
I seek the child of September.
I ask your bountiful high seas, sweet and nautical,
I ask your land breeze that rouses from their ashes the
                                        /grandfather words, .
I ask your East trade winds, crazed with Greek fables,
I retrace, from downstream, the river of my history
and I hear on the foamy delta of interlaced waves
                        —Bull Shark!—
'Tigrones!' clamor the natives, fleeing
in their canoes. And the pirate
shouting from the ship's boom: Bull Shark!
                        Bull Shark!
They sniff out from miles away the smell of pitch

---

81. *devonica* – Devonic period

and know they are the ships of death
the tortured thrown overboard,
the carrion of the hanged
those stabbed boarding other vessels, whose blood
fills with vertiginous fins the tragic blue.

John Davis went in with them by river
and crossed the Lake in bongo and fell upon sleeping Granada.
The bell towers sounded the alarm
but already the smoke of the fires
lifted crowns of vultures above the destroyed city.
Thus we came to know the unmistakable noise of empires:
the iron
the crackle of cities
and the ashen howl of dogs.
Because it comes
          and goes. 'And it is very agile in the water
this butcher.' Like l'Olonnais,
who also crossed the river
with his cohort of cetaceans.
This is the one who split the prisoners in two with a single stroke
                                                    /of the sword.
And shouted: —'*Mort Dieu! Les espagnols me le payeront!*'
The sweet lady Inez of Quiros taken hostage through the jungle
in her wedding gown.
The pieces of lace in the thorns guided the Indians
and they mounted an ambush and cornered him
and they quartered him and burned him and spread to the wind
his ashes.
But it comes
          and goes.
500 cows for a lady, charged Davis,
150 for a gentleman, the illustrious Dampier
(terror has always been negotiable)
and he would write with beautiful script about our trees
and then would hang the prisoners from their branches.
But the lady already carried your seed in her womb
Carcharhinus leucas!
and gave her son to an Indian woman and the boy

became corsair, 'the son of the female shark
whose hunger is the friend of storms.'[82]
This was Gallardillo, he who took and burned Granada again,
he who sang romances while decapitating prisoners.
And thus was Coxon
And thus was Harris
And thus was Horatio Nelson (of the Trafalgar)
—the gold of the buckles of his shoes
was stolen from the crown of Our Lady—
And thus was Sharp
and Bourmano. Because it comes
        and goes.
In the family mansion, before the dawn
resounded the heavy knocker from the vestibule and voices
                                    /were heard
and the servants ran with oil lamps
and did not know dirty Ulysses,
the son —prisoner of Coxon, the corsair—
ten years enslaved on the Caribbean Islands,
muscular, lean, with the mark of misadventure.
And his hand cut off by his own will
to erase the fiery brand of his owner.
—'Of the sharks
and of their incredible voracity I marveled with good reason.'
—says Acosta in his history.

4

Deep in the Nicaraguan country
on the hill by the river,
old Captain Samuel Shepherd
puts out, like an inner twilight, the rusty
lamp and enters the night
dragging his feet. Eternally
deluded, he smiles at the returning dream:
        High-keeled ships

---

82. *Isidoro Duchase, Conde de Lautremont: 'Cantos de Maldoror.*

lights on the bridges,
hoarse voices
of the helmsmen,
Scandinavian, Germanic, Saxon tongues,
boats from Britain
with Hindu crewmen
and old Karol with his fuming pipe
fidgeting his hand.
In the cemetery of Greytown lies genteel Elizabeth
puritan and pale. The two children
also parted to the ancient seas.
Oh, harsh land! Noxious flutes
rose up like serpents, twining and tangling.
Jungles resurrect from their tombs to smother
that which your hands erected. Mayan cities
under your rivers. Febrile ports,
dredges, customs houses, flagpoles of the consular assets
assimilated by the vegetation, nests
of constricting roots, grasses,
and under the grasses, headstones:

> *Elizabeth Cross*
> *1830-1866*
> *Devoured by the shark*

In a small box, like a fetus
her hand and her delicate skull.

5

Aldebaran[83] does not shine. None
of the constellations of the lover,
only the wasp nest of the Furies and the tail
of the Dragon, crepitate. You have turned

---

83. *Aldebaran* - Bull's Eye, fixed star in constellation of Taurus

another page of your history.
You have earned your freedom and again the sinister fin rakes
/your waters.

In the penumbra of the port, the Filibusters make their rowing
/approach.
The white city that you love
will see again its dawn opened at the edge of a knife.
Mothers will substitute the stars with their woes
and those shot down will once again open their arms against the
/wall of the night.
I weep for the sons of September,
Isidora, Blanca, Guadalupe,
they enter the great hall of the mansion seized by the usurper.
The light from the window illuminates Walker's pale face.
(Tomorrow it will be another face —because it comes and goes—)
They have implored mercy for those condemned to death.
(They keep on imploring.)
It is the same greenish light of the deep waters
and they do not hear the cruel words of the foreigner
they only see his cold eyes —*Carcharhinus leucas*— the impassible
/pupil.
In vain they tried to rebuild their paradise!
The moon returned
and found her kisses in ruins!

6

—On the anniversary of the victory
the corpulent dominator of the island
asked me about the cetacean
—'*Carcharhinus nicaraguensis,*'
—But it is not from here —I told him—.
It copulates in the bitter waters
and returns to the sweet waters.
And he touched my arm. —'I am interested
in everything you would tell me.'
But it was he who spoke.

He spoke to me of the sea.
—'I swam eight hours in the solitary waters
celebrating my birthday,'—he said. (The solitude of the ocean
equals the solitude of the multitudes).
His archaic profile, bearded
like the golden mask of Agamemnon
floating in this mediterranean where Poseidon does not dominate
but Hurricane
the god Papagayo[84] with eye of storm.
—It's not Nicaraguan? —he asked again.
—It comes and goes, I said. —It exploits
its power to adapt. It plunders
in a usurped kingdom.
And he spoke again of the sea.
He was seated with his plate on his knees
shelling the shrimp with expert fingers.
'Later he wiped from his head the salty sea foam
that had left the sea sterile.'[85]
And he came forth from the waves, strengthened by Solitude.
Utopia with its lash.
—I am inspired by this land —he said,
and the vivacious eye, inquisitive, asking about the cetacean
of the sweet waters.
And below lurking from the depths,
the other gaze,
the implacable eye
that 'dominates the doleful place, fierce and desolate.'[86]

---

84. *Papagayo wind* - The Papagayo wind is a north to northeasterly wind which periodically blows through the gap in the mountain ranges of Central America in which Lake Nicaragua is located. It is named for the Gulf of Papagayo on the Pacific coast in this region. The wind is stronger than the trade winds which normally blow here. It is notable for causing a pronounced increase in upwelling of cooler, nutrient-rich waters on the Pacific coast which in turn supports an abundance of sea life. The wind and upwelling are together referred to as a Papagayo event. (Wikipedia)
85. *Homer:* 'Odyssey.'
86. *John Milton:* 'Paradise Lost.'

7

We were born at the crossroads. Bridge
over volcanoes. Through here pass the dominators and the
/dominated.
The persecuted and the persecutors.
Peoples of the North came to the door of your house.
Peoples of the South entered your bedroom. You are the son
of the Exodus and like you the pilgrim
trees cross your jungles. Red flowers
left on your paths by Malinches
                    —They come from Anahuac
Black flowers left in your mountains by jaguars
stained by the moon
                    —They transport Mayan legends
and birds pass —emigrants of the Zodiac—
                    —garble of the Chibcha tongues
fabricating with architect beaks
nests round as the circles of the cosmos.
Here meet butterflies and tempests.
Here, like birds and tongues, come
migratory fish, dreamers
of routes. fish —mysterious exiles— species
that crossed from island to island so much silence
till they reach this intimate sea in the bosom of your Country!
See the archaic Gaspar, with his dentate alligator mouth,
with the armor of his scales impenetrable
—palimpsest of the obscure Mesozoic—
come from the North to archive your waters.
See the silvery Shad of the South.
Or the immense Saw-fish[87]
'With his ferocious sword full of fangs
that I have seen so large
that a pair of oxen
have ample cargo in such a fish.'[88]

---

87. *Sword Fish* - (Salas Estrada, 2002, p. 249) LATIN NAME: *Pristis pecti-*
     natus, OTHER NAMES: Pez sierra.
88. *Oviedo:* Natural History.

See in your waters those that dominated by their ferocity
and those that dominated by their adaptation
                    (because they were like us
                    sons of dialogue and sons of protest)
those that climb the rivers,
in colors that the drowned would dream of
                    —Guapotes,[89] Mogas, Mojarras,[90] Laguneros—
Those that are descended from salt
                    —Guabinas,[91] Sardines, Sabaletes[92]—
wet birds with no song!
But, behold! The velocity and the power
—*Carcharhinus leucas*— Latin of rough 'rr's'
for their sandpaper skin; five rows of teeth,
elastic, untiring in aggression, and in his eye
cold
seas of all the tyrannies.

            ...Then they flee.
The Machaca[93] sink into the sand:
the Catfish[94] bristles. The Shad jump.
They flee...

---

89. *Guapotes - Parachromis managuensis* is a cichlid native to Nicaragua
    in Central America: the scientific name means "from Managua" (as in
    Nicaragua's capital city). It is a food fish and is also found in the aquari-
    um trade where it is variously known as: the jaguar cichlid, managuense
    cichlid or managua cichlid, guapote tigre, Aztec cichlid, spotted guapote
    and jaguar guapote. ...The species is a carnivorous, highly predatory fish.
    (Wikipedia)
90. The mojarras are a family, Gerreidae, of fishes in the order Perciformes.
    Mojarras are a common prey and bait fish in many parts of the Caribbean
    including the South American Coast and Caribbean islands. ..Mojarra is
    also commonly used in Latin American countries as a name for various
    species of the Cichlid family including tilapia. (Wikipedia)
91. *Guabinas* - Hoplias malabaricus. (wolf fish)
92. Sabaletes (Salas Estrada, 2002, p. 249) LATIN NAME: *Dorosoma chave-*
    si.
93. *Machaca*- (White & Simon, 2007, p. 75) LATIN NAME: *Brycon guate-*
    *malensis (*Regen).
94. *Bagre* - (Salas Estrada, 2002, p. 248) LATIN NAME: *Bagre marinus.*

Oh, Thanatos![95]
Then you also lift your eyes
and seek the ship
drunken from routes.
'Alone on the deserted dock (on this September morning)
you look toward the entrance of the port, you look toward the
/Indefinite.'[96]

The ship arrives from afar and rejuvenates your heart.
The horizons summon you with their watery stars.
It is you —oh, stranger!— the foreigner
standing, on the prow,
nearing the adventure and the promise.
Vividly the slim keel
cuts time and the sea opens in two parts for your exodus.
Who are you fleeing from?
-In your heart you carry your land.
And wherever you go you transport your exiles.
From whom do you flee?
        —And I turned my face.
And I saw in the foaming wake the ominous shadow:
'Though laden with sails the ship be
—says Oviedo—
the shark is always by its side.'

Granada, Great Lake 1983

Coda

*'The boy went down to the river to bathe when a great fish jumped
from the water that wanted to devour him. Tobias shouted, but the
angel said to him: —'Grab the fish by the gills and hold on tight.'
And the boy overpowered the fish and dragged it to dry land. Then*

---

95. *Thanatos* - The Greek poet Hesiod established in his *Theogony* that
    Thánatos is a son of Nyx (Night) and Erebos (Darkness) and twin of
    Hypnos (Sleep).(Wikipedia).
96. Fernando Pessoa: 'Oda Maritima'.

the angel said to him: 'open the fish, take out the gall bladder, the
heart and the liver and throw away the intestines, because its gall
bladder, its heart and the liver will give you remedy.'

Tobias 6:1-5

NOTE: For Nicaraguans, September is the patriotic month, and Cuadra, in the Seven Stanzas of his poem, retraces the principle 'paintings' of the dramatic history of his people, converting the Shark in the symbol of Evil that comes and goes,' predator and messenger of destruction and murder.

The child devoured by the shark is 'the son of September,' the Nicaraguan, and the whole poem is a persecution against this sweet water 'Moby Dick', that nests in the Great Lake and that goes out to sea and returns, representing the aggression of imperialism and greed of all the signs.

Stanza 4: Greytown or San Juan del Norte, port of Nicaragua to the Atlantic during the splendor of the Transit (before the Panama Canal), now a dead city devoured by the jungle.

Stanza 6: Conversation with Fidel Castro in Managua.

The Epigraph of the poem suggests the weapon to combat the shark and the Coda seems to decipher the evil and good of the Shark, some of whose innards are useful, but others should be thrown to the outer night.

OCTOBER

SONG OF SPAIN

to Felix Grande

Antiphony

'Rainy October, copious year.'

Month of South-west gales, month of speeches. The last month of rains and the first of language.

'Memory stretches away sluggishness in October
from its habitual melancholy.
Speaks of genealogy.
And the crests of the sons of something clash
with those of the sons of no-one.
October, is a month of speeches:
zealous grandmothers darn the tears of the last names,
overly-solicitous grandfathers cover with rhetoric
the old capital sins of the race.
Still the jungles, the tyrannies and the distances
keep immense pieces of silence
but October loosens the tongue and weaves nations
from a seamless brotherhood.
—PAC

Around October 4 is produced the 'Cord of Saint Francis:' the Southern winds clash with the Northern and Eastern in an imposing battle of lightening and thunder, and the weather stays 'stuck in water.' Whole weeks of waters: rains, mists, heavy showers, squalls, violent gusts of wind and rain, or simply *"cat fluff (rain)."*

'Sun with beards, wind with waters.'
'Sun in mourning, damned downpour.'
'New moon thunder, nine days wet.'
Afternoons and nights of cold humidity; early mornings of piquant suns and refulgent blues.

At month's end a multitude of yellow flowers open on the edges of the roads. Yellow also —over green— the Sardinillo.[97]

Southern breeze and nostalgic.

---

97. *Sardinillo – family of Acacia tree*

October

'Children of the world, here is
Mother Spain with her womb on her shoulders;
here is our teacher with her canes,
here is mother and teacher,
cross and wood, because she gave you height,
vertigo and division and addition, children...'

Cesar Vallejo
(*'Spain take this chalice from me.'*)

1

'The white-bearded Spanish grandfather
points out a series of illustrative portraits;'
This is don Gil —the Extramaduran— son of Gil
goat herder. He crossed the sea
when Cipango, Cathay and the legendary Antilles
dissipated their myth and gave passage
among taunts and curses of sailors
to the immense uncharted land
where everything was different
and everything was possible.

—Son of a bitch he who called Castile of Gold
this land of swamps, and crazy
the Genovese, drunk with stars,
who painted little birds
and savory airs where I contracted mountain leprosy.
He believed he would find in the Indies a fief for a kingdom.
He died on a cot of sticks in Tustega
surrounded by his ten entrusted Indians
and by Josephine Potoy, his Indian mistress,

dreaming of his return to Spain
with gold and pearls, heralded by fame
in a court he only knew in troubadour song.

You wept, silent, clay lover,
barely mistress of bedroom words
—those necessary—
for a discerning love:
'Nugo': my man. 'Noji': your woman.
'Naneya': the children. And the Registrar writing down:
'Sancho, his son; Santiago, his son;
Josepha, his daughter. And don Gil his first born
Who now girds the sword.'

They later opened the old cedar trunk
as the quill writes:
'One travel hood, ordinary, with scarlet fringe.'
'One black cape, old, (the one he thought
to wear, with his satin doublet, to enter the palace).'
'One yellowed vest lined with linnet,'
'Some old black trousers'
'Two torn tunics of damask.'
'One buckler,'
'One notched sword (the one that he thought
to show in testimony to his heroic exploits)'
and 'the old feathered hat' that now
smiling through tears, puts on
don Gil, his first born.

2

This don Gil did not love the sea of numerous noises
nor did he build a foundation on nostalgias
but planted his feet like roots on land of bread for the taking
and said that one of his feet wore big Extremaduran shoes[98]

---

98. *Extremadura,(Spain) i.e. His shoes were handed down from Spain.*

and the other, Indian, sower of corn-fields.
And he was territorial like a tree
and founded civilizations with oxen
—the first oxen in Beremejo and Morro
that opened their first furrows in a brown and virgin May—
('And the most solemn triumphs of the greatness of Rome—
were not as acclaimed as those oxen that day.')

And he did not love the sword, origin of groans
but what rested his heart in the immense
Nicaraguan nights, whose stars
imagine other fables
and dance to other music.
And his ears did not hear birds from Provence[99]
—that don Gil, his father, mocked in the chronicles—
but Chorotegan birds in name and in song:
pretty nuris
tucans
piticocos
pijules
and paujiles
and that brown tremolo bird of feathers of clay
and the guis of strident yellow morning song
and the fall of the lemon in his patio
as if the sun threw him his autograph.
He married a Castillian widow, doña Ubalda, said to him:
—Petition, Gil, the King, that which your father
won with his battles;
but he watched his cattle and said:
—From King and from fire, faraway.
And thus, his Castile was his bed
and his oxen, Castillian
and his pigs and hens, Castillian
and his roses, Castillian
and his wine, Castillian
—What his mother called 'Castillian Silian'

---

99. *Provence*, France.

and his Indians 'Silian tipotani' —fermented drink of the gods.—
when they served it on his table, on Castillian tablecloths.
This don Gil died of old age in the town he founded
hearing the bells of his church toll in his agony
and he saw from his bed the townspeople
invading his house with tears and prayers
and he turned to doña Ubalda and said:
—Listen, woman, my bells mourn for me. I die accomplished.
I did not found a Lordship but a neighborhood.

3

The inheritor was his offspring, Don Gil the Third
young golden-beard and tall.
His mother doña Ubalda
looked at him and said: —'I do not want
a grandson of a Conquistador to sleep his nobility among cows.'
And wrote to the Dean of Santiago de Leon of gentlemen,
                                              /his relative:
'I believe that in service to the Governor my son will exact
                                              /nobility.'
Well, log the youth with velvet doublet and cloak of finest wool,
catalog him in the Town Chapter; not a month as page
and the Justice will take his oath before a Christ pedestal over
                                              /a crimson cloth

—'They were three cloaked —said the page— well armed
with coats of mail, swords and bucklers
and don. Alonzo shouted:
Ah, don Luis! Weren't you perchance my friend?
and they stabbed him leaving him for dead.'

And to the ears of doña Ubalda came the name of the new tailor
installed in Leon with cloth from Cataluna
and ordered Pedro Campo, for the noble page,
a doublet of shimmering cloth
and to the Dean another letter: 'My dearest Uncle
I hope that in your shadow my son will have the writing

and manners and tongue of a gentleman.'
But once again boils the Town Chapter, 'and made the witness
/appear'
—the judge dictating to the scribe—
and he swore and did not deny before the Holy Christ
that 'he came to collect himself on the street of La Merced
—it was the day they celebrate the rejoicing of Saint Faust—
when that Juan Diaz, nervous man,
took out his sword and shouting improprieties,
repeatedly thrust his sword into doña Ana de la Cueva'
grandiose woman and of high parentage.
The case ended in the gallows. And the page wrote to his mother
with melancholy chest and mournful:
'Between quarrels, weapons and horses
the letters of the Dean slip away from me...'

...And so this don. Gil parted for Spain...

No sooner had he set foot on the ship and heard the naval winds
and the creak of ratchets and mizzen
that his heart opened from province to universe.

And he disembarked in the port of Seville.

And he went crazy for Spain.

And sailed in Cathedrals and Castles
—naves are of stone to transcend time—.

But 'I looked at the walls of my country
if once strong, now dilapidated'
and I hit the table with my fist
and called the militia lazy
the decline of the Empire
and swore by Pelayo of Cantabria[100]
by those of war, fierce Mars,

---

100. *Pelayo* - area of water that washes Spain's Northern Coast.

the famous Cid[101]
Wamba, the king of police nobility
And the Castillian Isabella who overcame Semiramis...
'Mocito[102] —said my uncle don Fadrique to me, just come
/to Madrid,—
put away your sword because here heroes abound!'

...And he was the Indian.

They saw the Indian feather under his hat
and a suspicious Jewish gleam in his doubloons.

My admiration rose to hear Lope
and I went to the corral and he gave me in the face
the disdain of don Bela.
(Oh, crazy empire. There from the sea
your glory is the mestizo and the new Christian,
here the cleansing of blood and the old Christian!)
And he knew the ridicule of the Court.

And he knew the solitude of the Inca.

And the silence of Spain.

---

101. *El Cid* - Rodrigo Díaz de Vivar (1043– 1099), was a Castilian nobleman,
military leader, and diplomat. Exiled from the court of Alfonso VI of
León and Castile, El Cid went on to command a Moorish force consisting
of Muladis, Berbers, Arabs and Malians, under Yusuf al-Mu'taman ibn
Hud, Moorish king of the northeast Al-Andalus city of Zaragoza, and
his successor, Al-Mustain II. After the Christian defeat at the Battle of
Sagrajas, El Cid was recalled to service by Alfonso VI, and commanded
a combined Christian and Moorish army, which he used to create his own
fiefdom in the Moorish Mediterranean coastal city of Valencia. Rodrigo
Díaz was educated in the royal court of Castile and became the *alférez*,
the chief general, of Alfonso VI, and his most valuable asset in the fight
against the Moors. (Wikipedia)
102. *Mocito* – nickname for 'moso', farm hand.

4

Don Gil returned so dejected
—despain he called his disillusion—
that his uncle, don Fadrique, now in the nave, gave him a book
and told him: —Read Cervantes. No disillusion exhausts Spain.
And Cervantes filled
his 'hours of grief and sadness.'

There he learned that history
is not yesterday but tomorrow.
And his heart occupied his center once again
that is the center of the world
and between Sancho and Quijote
he litigated 'the long dispute between tradition and invention,
order and adventure.'

'Liberty, Sancho, my friend,
is the most precious gift that the heavens
have given to men.'

And he ran aground
—his foot anxious to open a path—. And he closed the book
and said: Take courage, don Gil!
America is the third wave of Quijote!

And so was this don Gil, neighbor of Leon of Nicaragua.
His headstone is covered with the ash of a volcano.
His face was chiseled by the language.
And he was the father of don Gil
—settler of Piura
Grandfather of don Gil
—settler of Quito
Great-Grandfather of don Gil
—soldier of Bolivar.

1987

NOTE: The poet does not sing to Spain but decomposes the specter of 'the Spanish' —and the love of Spain— in a succession of 'Gil's. (The discoverers of Nicaragua were, Christopher Columbus on Atlantic side and Gil Gonzalez Davila on the Pacific, but the characters of the poem, —although historic—, 'were chiseled by the language.')

The person who tells the song is a Darian character: 'The white-bearded Spanish grandfather of *Prosas Profanas.* Through him we see that *'the most Spanish act of Spain was not the conquest, but independence,'* as written elsewhere by the singer of 'October.'

NOVEMBER

THE DEATH OF THE WARRIOR

To Fernando Quinones

ANTIPHONY

'Time is wind,' says the mariner's refrain. After the predominance of the Southerlies break the Northerly winds that cut the winter rains, installing the dry season. Fresh airs. In the lake region, the predominant winds are called 'Breezes'[103] or 'Lestes'[104] that dry up the mud of the paths. The proverb teller turns aerial:

'Wind that stays for dinner/ blows all night.'

'Wind that lies down at nightfall/ rises at dawn.'

'The Macaw sings, and the weather changes[105].'

Scissor-tailed swallows arrive: rosy breasts and long tails that cut the air.

Large worms appear in the bark of the trees.

The Fish-hook (or Scorpio) is no longer visible.

The wind lights the stars like embers. 'When the owl sings, the Indian dies / this is not really true, but it happens.'

---

103. *Brisas* - Showers
104. *'Lestes'* - Easterlies
105. *Guas* – (Gargiullo, Magnuson, & Kimball, 2008, pp. 98-99) *LATIN NAME: Ara ambiguus*- Great Green Macaw or *Ara macao* - Scarlet Macaw

NOVEMBER

The dead guerilla was carried to his tent.
Horsemen who were questioned returned from the dusty roads.
'Dead!...Dead!' —they repeated, increasing among the brambles
the vagrant whimper of November.

Hands that apprehended the ellipse in clay
and fixed perpetually the perpetual unrest
now bind the white shrouds of thread
shooing the buzzing blue of the wing of the fly.
But a little blood, an insistent drop,
opening up,
like the damp eye of the spring,
extended slowly over the chest its purple stain.

The potters watched the growing rose
overstaying its time,
flowing when the Definitive
was already marked as Inevitable by their harsh cries.
Oh! disheveled faces, oh! darkened
silences next to the dry clay, unfinished
—amphorae suspended between the poor dejected hands—
and outside, where November
passes with its hostile and funereal dust,
only shadows, memories say
the sad horsemen that return.
How many had a name
—shoots from the dense vine
endured—
for the hot canon of his revolver,
for his hand

powerful
calling forth fire,
or his shout
that filled the calendar with battles!

The rose grows from lives: stains the thread
with blood that now is not his own! There they spill
his last syllable, those who no longer have
songs in the night; those who now guard
with fear their weapons stalking a sound
or footsteps
of the enemy that only for him, with foreign gestures, they
                                              /confronted,
or those
—the unharmed, the forgers of April—
that come down to the fiestas with his name
written in hope!
roses of the people!, the potters
touch time and see its purple stain,
duration that can no longer be sustained,
silence that invades and erases the region
while they weep, ay!, and their hands
become mechanical to turn the black amphorae of the mortal
                                              /month.

Let the clay enclose its history in signs,
may November dry the clay with its howling moan.
The dead guerilla was carried to his tent
and only one slow red rose repeats
in the Indian amphorae.

1938/ 1950

NOTE: This poem is the oldest in this book and one of the first
       songs to the likeness of Sandino in Nicaraguan literature,
       though the author has expressed – does not refer to the death
       of Sandino, but of Miguel Angel Ortez, the valiant young
       guerilla who enthused all the youth of these years and who

earned a handsome sonnet by Manolo Cuadra, companion of Pablo Antonio in the Vanguard Movement.

The poem 'November,' however, more than a laudatory song is the creation of the myth of abandonment and disillusion when 'the man' who sustains, with his courage and personality, an epoch or a cause succumbs. The elegy is wrapped in the funereal atmosphere of November, month of the departed in Catholic Liturgy and of leaves that fall...

DECEMBER

OUR LADY OF THE BLUE SHAWL

To Mother Ana

ANTIPHONY

December is the second Nicaraguan spring: the white Spring, with its light and fresh airs that give the month its charm. Snow does not exist in the tropics, but nature invents it: White clouds like flocks of Sheep. Clouds of doves. White flowers of the Madronos. White flowers of Easter. Cotton plantations. And the red letter of the year that ends around a cradle, of a manger: the large red flowers of the Poinsettias and of the 'Flames of the Forest.'

Month of Mary: the Virgin and the Mother. Around the 8th, the 'Purissimas'[106] novena dedicated to the Immaculate Virgin that ends the day of the 'Griteria'[107] (at seven in the evening). In all the streets and paths of Nicaragua the people shout 'Who causes so much joy?' and the people respond: —'The Conception of Mary!'

Later, the tradition of the Posadas. On any path, in any neighborhood you can encounter Joseph and Mary riding a donkey or a mule asking for lodging. Children accompany them with lanterns.

And Christmas. The nativity or manger scenes.
Infant month.
Month of candies and sweets.
Month of flutes, tambourines, ocarinas, and reed whistles.
Month of fireworks: rockets, firecrackers and fireworks.
Month of stars.
And the brief rains that fall are called 'cabanuelas.'

---

106. *Purissimas* – Means 'Most Pure' and refers to the Immaculate Conception of Mary
107. *Griteria* – 'The Shouting', another name for the Purissima celebration

DECEMBER

'There began the work of destruction
in the middle of the village, the misery of all
the world. There they raised the good of the word
of God, the message came from the mouth
of God. There will come a white creature
from the heavens named the Virgin Woman.
Her house has seven red stars.'
XV Book of the Vatican of the Thirteen [Katunes.[108]]

CHILAN BALAM DE CHUMAYEL[109]
(*Trad. A. Mediz Bolio*)

Barefoot you place your foot over the old Sundays
to cross over the river of tears:
your countrymen
learn this step —an exodus—,
the women with their baskets, airily
jump behind You, raising slightly
with wise fingers, their petticoats. The men,
clumsy in the dance, watch the rocks

---

108. *Katunes* - A k'atun or k'atun-cycle is a unit of time in the Maya calendar equal to 20 tuns or 7,200 days (Wikipedia).
109. The Books of Chilam Balam are handwritten, chiefly 18th-century Mayan miscellanies, named after the small Yucatec towns where they were originally kept, and preserving important traditional knowledge in which indigenous Mayan and early Spanish traditions have coalesced. Written in the Yucatec Maya language and using the Latin alphabet, the manuscripts are attributed to a legendary author called Chilam Balam, a *chilam* being a priest who gives prophecies and *balam* a common surname meaning 'jaguar'. Some of the texts actually contain prophecies about the coming of the Spaniards to Yucatan while mentioning a *chilam* Balam as their first author (Wikipedia).

that the current of time polishes. And they pass.
                    Where
do we go, behind You, Lady of the blue shawl?

Behind the footprint of heroes
our thoughts have been made blood.
We have wanted to build the 'here'
—a wide, a high
paradisiacal 'here' never satisfied—
and we relieve our arms, tired
from sustaining the starry canopy,
the infinite weight of the finite.
And we call to the marble pillar to detain our weariness.
We call to the bronze. Or to the word
that also, by its own weight, falls.

Behind the footprint of lovers
our feelings have also been made blood.
Memory is a place full of tears.
So many times we try
to secure the instant
…but it passes! And the fist of dust my hand gathers
was a pupil. A glance. That is death:
that which subsists like a star and is no more!

Not in my death
but in that of the one I love
is death revealed. Botticelli
wets his brushes in the weeping
and his Venus —lachrymose—
does not revive mortal absence.
…Rains in Tikal and we think of the sweet young Mayan women
offered to the god fearless of time.
Not in my end but in the end of love
does death rebel. In the song that hushes
but also in that which remains.

We were, then, seated by the torrent
and there flowed a fleeting crepuscular theory of trees,

breezes, kisses, thoughts
and jubilant maidens
with perishable roses among their years.
Not only when I remember my death (which is future)
but when I forget the past
I am my death!

Lady: for many years my crowded heart
filled with faces and words
and I filled, in my time, my song
of the people. I ran the risk
of not being heard
because poetry is also a piece of poverty.
I ran the risk
of seeing my heart empty and deserted
when Power placed his foot over the mouth of the humble.
I thought that my epitaph
would be equivalent to the beggar's.
Did you not hear Eliphaz, Bildad, and Zophar?
They were my friends, but now
turning their backs, they curse me.
And the interrogatives multiply.
And the hawks in the plain.

Vultures. Why that moan
of the innocent? Why that maternal lament
like a sword? And why the tyranny, the opprobrium,
the cruelty, the leopard's eye of my brother
who tortures
and the impeccable lime whitening his sepulcher?...

In the night the wind, that blows where it wills,
forms words that whisper: 'If your faith is vulnerable
it is because it exists.' But the interrogations return
come back to crown me with thorns.
And again the Wind: 'The scandal of the world
is not suffering but liberty.'
And then we read the Scripture.

And at the edge of night the Angel descends to drive away the
/stone
that covers memory, presence, and promise.
—Because there is no utopia only Resurrection—

Lady: the poet reproaches the angels who are often confused
and do not know if they walk among the living or the dead.
/Narrow is
the door that separates the Farewell from the Encounter.
I weep for absence and believe he has parted,
but my hand still takes hold of my father's hand
and my father his father's hand.
You have not let go of history.
Hand in hand you are taken by the hand of Abraham,
/of the Promise.
Hand in hand you are taken by the hand of Quetzalcoatl
/of the Omen,
and in middle of the ages Christ extends his hands
and the Preterite and the Future are united in Christ.

From that glorious procession I descend and in her I march.
The most subtle essences of my song come from those hands
that transmit agape.
Now we come behind You, Lady.

Who would say that your foot —descending time—
would touch my exsanguinated land?
My friend, the countryman,
remembered that he had not fed the animals
And 'he just left in the direction of the trees of Coyol'[110]
when lightning shined
'—DA
DATTA! A century of prudence
will not silence our truth!—

---

110. *Coyol* - (Gargiullo, Magnuson, & Kimball, 2008, p. 2) LATIN
NAME:Acrocomia aculeate, FAMILY: A. vinífera, OTHER NAMES:
Spiny palm,

'I raised my eyes —he told me— and over the little Morisco tree
I saw the resplendent cloud
and over the cloud, her bare feet.
—Could I be asleep? —I said within myself.
But blinking I saw that the border of the gown
                                    /folded the leaves of the Morisco,
and I wanted to speak to her but my voice was a tomb.
Then She smiled and I was able to ask her
—What is Your name, Lady?
and She, with the sweetest voice that I had ever heard,
answered me: —Mary.'

Lady, you have placed Jacob's ladder between your heaven and my
                                    /earth
and we together have come behind You to December: end and
                                    /beginning.
I speak of You, the woman among all women
Whose face most resembles that of Christ.
When you spoke with Bernardo
Your hand played with the tassel of the shawl.
Your hand that opens for us the portal of the night
and we see —through tears— that the sepulcher is empty.

We have come behind You to Bethlehem. And is born
(which is to die) and dies
(which is to be born) he who redeems time.
'By Him life is transformed, does not end.'
By Him is reborn the To Be and Being (the time
that he made me and that which we made). We recuperate
the ephemeral. The boy, the youth, the poet
who died so many times.
All of life in its successive deaths
returns by Him. The angels move the heavy stone.
And by Him the law of gravity is inverted:
we go falling
in a space of sweetest heights.
Falling in the blue. We go
falling like the Fish

—that when it dies, floats—
in the abysmal blue that the angels keep.

Managua, Nicaragua 1984
Austin, Texas 1986

NOTE: The poem closes the year with a song of resurrection. 'There is no utopia but resurrection' —says the poet. And Jose Maria Gonzalez Ruiz writes: 'If in the struggle for some better situations in society Christians contribute something specifically, it is precisely this: the enthusiasm for the material even to believe in resurrection, and at the same time, making relative all movement produced before the end of history.' The poem is, therefore, Paulesque, as was another great Nicaraguan poem: *'The Song of War of the Things'* by Joaquin Pasos (Paul: Romans 8, Corinthians 15, and Thessalonians.)

But the sacred and confirming figure of the poem is Mary —'Janua Coeli', portal of heaven—, whose footsteps reinforce the footprints of Christ, opening to man the secret path of Time to Eternity. (The poet in one writing had said: 'Modern man has depreciated the word 'eternity' by lack of imagination'). And Mary appears in the poem in her manifestation in Cuapa (Chontales, Nicaragua) to a countryman, whose tale is woven with the verses of the poem and whose appearance opens with the explosion of thunder from 'Wasteland' by T. S. Eliot:

—DA
DATTA!

In its double meaning and sound of thunder (that was produced in the apparition) and from admonition to love and to not keep silent. From the lips of Bernardo, the country seer, Cuadra heard the delicate detail of the hand of Mary, playing with the fringe of the shawl while she spoke, that gives title to the poem.

The epigraph gathers a surprising and mysterious Marian prophesy of the CHILAM BALAM DE CHUMAYEL.

TIKAL is the lovely Mayan city of Peten, Guatemala.

Eliphaz, Baldad and Zofar are the friends of Job.

'The poet (who) reproaches the angels who are confused and do not know whether they w alk among the living or the dead' is Rilke.

'Her whose face most resembles that of Christ': Translation of Dante's verse: '...ch'a Cristo piu si somiglia' (Paradise, Son 32).

'By Him life transformed, does not end': Verse from SANTUS of the Mass for the Dead.

It is important to point out the theological conception of the Resurrection —not only the 'to be' but of the 'being' that illuminates the poem— as in complete defeat of Death. That is to say, that which Christ, Son of Man rescues is not just the person, but also his cosmic context indissolubly joined to her now that Christ, besides being God the Savior is God the Creator. Saint Paul writes that the universe groans like the pains of the birth awaiting its liberation.'

Final Song to Our Lady

If I name you in the day
the day fills me with joy
and is called Mary
total joy
conceived without original stain.

Also when in the gente morning
breeze my plea I raise on wings
the dawn is the submissive
slave to your dictation
and your smile ignites all the valley.

All the valley singing
is concreted in the lips of the rose
and perfume orbiting
your delightful wheel
at the same time showing its airy measure.

For this we say to you
Queen of Time and of your law, Lady
because in Cana we see you
advance the hour
and at your request night becomes dawn.

Your voice is that which initiates
the mystic groan of the jasmine
the nostalgia of violins
and is music and caress
and is song and is love and is delight.

But your look is more:
Jacob's ladder which I prefer
to heaven lifted
from star to star
to climb to the reign of the Lamb.

When the Lord told you
—hanging by love on the wood—
'Mother behold your son.'
I was the inheritor
of the Mother of the True Son.

Thus in the pain
—if the night closes in weeping—
you incline with love
and your mantle covers me
the one you took, Mother, to the Holy Mount!

Return, then, to Bethlehem
my sinful life
to be reborn in your portal,
and then your hand, holy and maternal
opens the door of the Supreme Good:
leave it, Lady,
ajar now
and in the hour of our death. Amen.

APPENDIX A

THE SONS OF SEPTEMBER

by Pablo Antonio Cuadra

It has now been some years ago – when our group of 'the Vanguard' launched nationalistic manifestos and submerged itself in the popular sources seeking the roots of our mestizo culture in order to nourish and produce a Nicaraguan literature. I wrote a poem in which I wanted to summarize —with a poetic language as yet insecure— the irony and the drama of being Nicaraguan. The poem is entitled 'The Son of September' and says:

> *I fought with don Gil in the first*
> *Nicaraguan war. As a boy I was an indian,*
> *and Spanish and in unison they wounded me.*
> *I have a bilingual shout in both graves*
> *because they shot me with arrows in the*
> *white side and bullets*
> *in my brown skinned pain.*
>
> *Much later, in '21, they battered*
> *my two fertile halves in dreams:*
> *ORDER with the king, and I was hanged;*
> *ADVENTURE —democratic— shoved*
> *from joyful liberty and...shot down!*
> *Lovely tomb September for flowers!*
>
> *Passing to easier bloods, the gunpowder*
> *resounded later in dualistic funerals:*
> *I inured myself liberal to the grave*
> *with speeches in Leon. But in Granada*
> *they buried me in green and with drums.*
> *Historic is my death in two versions!*

282   PABLO ANTONIO CUADRA

Today as poor I fight with the rich:
I am boss or I declare myself worker
my Union in general strike.
Two-headed coffin carries my remains,
so when I want freedom I kill myself
And when I am free I die!

In this first visceral probing, the Nicaraguan I found inside of me, was a dual being with two dialoging and belligerent halves.

The poem was written in my school years. From a window of my study in the Central American College – I contemplated day by day a gallery of great statues of stone sculpted in remote ages by Indian ancestors. These statues repeat in an obsessive manner the theme of the human being with an animal adhered to his back, forming a sculptural unity of monstrous beauty. Sometimes the animal seems to creep upon the man or the woman, or overburden them in a Dantesque torture. On other occasions, the animal —alligator, serpent, eagle, coyote, jaguar— is still more integrated to the human body in such a way that the face of the man appears within the fauces of the animal forming one dual countenance. Other times the animal creeps only upon the human head as signifying a double mentality.

These monumental sculptures speak to me of a mythical and mysterious conception of the 'double ego' or 'vital alter ego' that surely signified a religious movement or animist magic, forged by a very ancient culture, perhaps Mangue/Chorotega, or perhaps before, that had original and irradiating focus —according to most archaeologists— the region of the Nicaraguan lakes; dualist conception (of the 'other self') that extended its influence to very distant regions in the North and South of America: as far as Mexico and Guatemala —in the pre-Aztec and pre-Mayan cultures— to the North, and as far as Colombia (in the Chibchas of Saint Augustine), Ecuador (in Manabi), Peru, (in Chavin of Huanta), the Amazons (in the regress of the Tronbetas), to the South.

This conception of the 'double ego' that Nicaragua produced —of which are only left to us the graphic texts of these sculptures, as also the extremely varied and surprising drawings of the ceramics of these ages— would thus signify belief in superior and inferior likeness of the human being, some ascribed to the soul —depicted in the protecting animal, a kind of inseparable guardian angel— and the others ascribed to the body...?

Archeologists perhaps someday will decipher the unknown. I only took that duality as a point of departure. And before my astonished poet's eyes, the 'I am other' of Rimbaud seems to me was made statue two thousand years before by the work of the primitive Nicaraguans.

On the other hand, the Chorotegas and the Nicaraguas tell in their traditions —they are the two superior cultures that dominated our country at the coming of the Spaniards— that when they left fleeing, exiled, from Mexico, their chiefs and their priests, or 'alfaquies', consulted their gods, and these ordered them to leave toward the South, advising them to only stop when they encountered in a lake, an island with two twin volcanoes (Ometepec).

The dual sign of the two volcanoes prophesied caused them to occupy Nicaragua. There they established themselves since the VIII Century of our era. And it is interesting to observe —in the mystery of this prophesy— that the new Indio-Hispanic history of Nicaragua also begins, exactly in front of these two volcanoes, with a dialogue: the conversation between the Nicaraguan Chief and the conqueror, Gil Gonzalez Davila in 1531.

There begins the clash and the fusion of the new duality. Two bloods, two cultures, next to the symbol of the two volcanoes, and in the land that had conceived humanity as a dramatic duality.

Would the Nicaraguan man be divided by doubt? indecisive? Because in the 'do' of (the word) 'doubt' also resides the same two of duality, says Ortega and Gasset. Will we always be —pushed by this destiny— defying rending dilemmas? Or is the Nicaraguan the fusion of antagonisms, the unification of contrasts?

We have been placed in a mediterranean center, in the navel of the New World.

In Nicaragua the flora and fauna of North America over-laps and joins —living together— with the flora and fauna of South America. The first dialogue begins with nature. In the Pre-Colombian Cultures here also unite the Chibchas and Pre-Incas of the South with the Toltecs and Nahuas of the North. An author has noted that even in vices Nicaragua was the umbilical center: tobacco came down South, and 'coca' came up North, meeting here in the middle..

The Spanish conquest also was carried out in Nicaragua uniting two currents: one from the North, driven by Mexico: and the other from the South, driven by Panama, currents that clash here, and of whose clash Nicaragua was formed in its limits and in its unity.

Later, the singular duality that divided Nicaragua in two localized partialities —East and West— producing the fairly original phenomenon in the history of America, of a country under the bicephalous governing of two cities —Leon and Granada— duality that ended upon finding solution in a new capital: Managua.

We are a country of only two seasons —winter— reign of mud —and summer— reign of dust, a dual scene that is aggravated by a landscape of lakes and volcanoes. Already Ruben called 'rough harmony' this antagonistic fusion of the potent ardor of our lands with the serene placidity of our waters.

The Nicaraguan is born in an angle of a 'Y', in a mediterranean vertex that obliges the incessant undertaking to unite, to fuse, and dialogue.[1]

Pablo Antonio Cuadra

---

1.   (Cuadra, El Nicaragüense, 1993; 13th edition 2004, pp. 15-18) (*See, also on dualism, the poem 'Pablo y Antonio,'* Poesia II. Ed.)

APPENDIX B

'El Nican-Nauat.'
'The Codex of Ashes (in the conversion of Nicaragua).

> *'Because I know that time is only time*
> *And place is always, and nothing more, than place*
> *And the actual is actual not more than a moment*
> *And nothing more in one place.'*

T. S. Eliot. 'Ash Wednesday'

I.

Long ago in the quotidian pain of the twilight
we wept to the Sun. The light entered
the dangerous territory of the darkness
where the immense Night, devourer of centuries,
no one knew which son would be engendered in its black marriage
                                                                                    /bed,

whether Death or Life.
Now the West is the port
where the Sun embarks to rescue from the shadows
other lands
other men
other dreams.
Now the twilight is landscape
(a scarlet king flees
from the burning of his empire in a day.)

Now, liberated from the god of the ordinary
I follow his itinerary. I imagine
my Indian caravels crossing a foreign world:
All history under lock and key

(the thousands of years they spend sailing toward Solid Land).
What do you say of love, of the infinite frustration,
of joy, of death
this other half born of other gods
and governing their lives by other stars?

I drew close to the preacher,
(Yesterday he spoke to me of Rome,
the Teotihuacan[2] from where the sun is born,
the holy city where the lamb devoured the wolf.

I drew close to Brother Poverty[3]
and the multitude surrounded me in the atrium of the hermitage
            —white like the inn of the moon—
and the hand of the 'alfaqui'
reached the brow of the King and traced upon it a cross of
                                                    /ashes.
        —Dust you are —he told me
(And I felt the trembling and the murmuring from the plaza.)
        —Dust I am —I thought.
With this dust God keeps on making the Cosmos.
With this oblivion man keeps making history.
What happens remains.
And I felt in the light layer of ashes the unsupportable weight
                                                    /of time.

---

2.   Teotihuacán was a city in pre-Columbian America. At the time it was
     most populated, it was the largest known city there...from about the 1st to
     5th century...The civilization and culture around this city is also called
     Teotihuacán. Its important position can be seen in various sites in Vera-
     cruz, and the area controlled by the Maya civilization. (Wikipedia)
3.   Brother Toribio de Benavente came among the twelve monks who formed
     the Franciscan apostalate destined to evangelize Mexico. For his holi-
     ness and poverty the Indians called him Brother Motolinia that means
     Brother Poverty. He came to Nicaragua and dialogued (converted) the
     Chief. Note by PAC

II

In two histories the great disk of fire divided the world.
There —in the other edge of the great Sea—
The Word, like the whispering insect,
goes fertilizing peoples and ages.
Buddha kills dragons and passions.
Socrates pursued ideas.
Strange clarities come to our minds
from the other side of this salty and blue wall.
But history here has a readjusted countenance;
unknown peoples speak dead languages
and they cross the straits of ice
from island to island
from shipwreck to shipwreck
to ignite the first word
in the immense continent of silence.
There Greece, there Rome, there Jerusalem.
Here the Olmecas fought with the giants
like the first peoples of the Book of the Christians.
Here Teotihuacan, the holy city
that Cain Tezcatiploca did not build, but Abel Quetzalcoatl;
Teotihuacan: the celestial city that offered butterflies to the gods.
Here Texcoco and his poet King
Netzahualcoatl:
nearing in the penumbra the Inventor of Self,
the Giver of Lives
hurling to him painful doubts
—interrogating arrows—
'Who, in truth, is your friend?
Can no one be at your side?
Who are you?
We seek you and perhaps we are next to You
like among the flowers
the invisible breeze.'

Woe! I have crossed under the weight of ashes
civilizations and seas.
From island to island I have navigated Myth and Utopia
And wherever I turn my eyes: ashes!

III

But there are footprints. In the ashes, footprints.
Footprints and deserts and portents
and the humble alfaqui with torn habit
gave me his hand and I crossed deserts
prophecies and deserts
until a silent town where a youth prayed.
She was there
not edified by Glory, nor by Fame.
No stranger to her sweet youth
but flowering of Herself,
Woman among all women.
Virgin and beautiful
beautiful and most pure
when surprise opened the rose of her hearing
and the Ineffable was expressed in word
and was born the most beautiful dialogue of human history.
A dialogue between Heaven and Earth.
Do not fear, says Heaven. And humility ascends
to the lips of God.

Has received the kiss
Has converted,
the inconceivable in conceivable.
A young woman encloses in her breast
the new creation of Man!
Eve, submissive, yields recovered Eden's key
Coatlicue[4] unclasps her belt of skulls

---

4.   The word "Coatlicue" is Nahuatl for "the one with the skirt of serpents". She is referred to variously as "Mother Goddess of the Earth who gives birth to all celestial things", "Goddess of Fire and Fertility", "Goddess of Life, Death and Rebirth", and "Mother of the Southern Stars", mother of Quetzalcoatl. She is represented as a woman wearing a skirt of writhing snakes and a necklace made of human hearts, hands, and skulls... Most Aztec artistic representations of this goddess emphasize her deadly side, because Earth, as well as loving mother, is the insatiable monster that consumes everything that lives. She represents the devouring mother, in whom both the womb and the grave exist. (Wikipedia) (See PAC's poem about Coaticue in.

and flees to the night of myths.
Produced are
the descent
and the ascent
of the Word
Truth is able to weep
and drink the milk from her breasts.
The Heir has been conceived
in a house
in a town
in a poverty no different from the poverty of our poor.
A God smaller than humility.
A God of God.
A Man.

Ashes.
Pollen.[5]

31 December, 1996

5. (Cuadra, Poesia I: 2003; pp. 267-270.)

APPENDIX C

Exvoto to the Guadalupana

by Pablo Antonio Cuadra

To Mary, the Governess of the Moon.
To the Mother of the Light: I begin to sing.
She peers through the window of the matutinal house.
Hear as song
I will invoke the sweet brown Archangel of tri-colored wings.
To You, oh, Holy Mary, the Best! To You, little one,
I sing interrupted by the silence of your humble eyes
and I tear from your hands the caress that I desire
when pain wanders through America
like a leaf from the tree melancholically uncertain,
like the butterfly dead in the path.

Ah! I find myself in the margin of history
like a fly on the edge of the cup consumed
and I make the effort to save for new generations
your smile forgotten in commercial struggles,
your embrace despised by the blind sons,
your voice that suffers the absence of sound.

Seek us, Lady, because we suffer the errors
of the ant in rainy days
when a drop of water
breaks the trajectory of the fixed path.
Because we are the small rubbish in the rivulet,
or the sole of the shoe flung around the neighborhood
or the useless persistence of the wheels mired in the mud.
Your face blankets the seriousness of the path.
Even so, where will the dreamers walk?

Clothe —oh, Lady!— with the edge of your mantle
the thoughts
cornered like children in the trembling of our voices:
because they are scattered like stones in the dust,
and well You may, who made the hill to flower,
resurrect from destruction our humble shacks.

Your foot knows the fatigue
of these walkers we see depart heavy laden.
The word of the poor You pronounced,
and here we gave you shelter, by the rustic bed,
by the ashen kitchen. You were watching
the food of the elderly, the sickness of the dispossessed,
the acquiescent smile of those who
'wait for the work of death.'
Why did you choose the Indian that we carry
in our eyes? Why did you seek the depth
of this blood, the origin of this permanence?

Oh! Pray for us, Lady,
You who speak with the sweetness of the faraway calf,
You who gaze with the infantile effort of the lamp
of the Tabernacle,
You who wait with the same incalculable desire
of herbs in drought for the water of winter.
You, who have heart like the countryside,
where all fragrances flower.

Because your gazes fly like wild doves,
because your hands are the embracing hammock,
the shadow of the Ojoche[6] and of the laurel,
the gourd of refreshing water,
the river found in the middle of the plain.
We will wrap your calls in the soul,

---

6. Ojoche trees - Brosimum alicastrum, are endemic to Central America
and grow in the forests of Northern Nicaraguan communities. Produces
Maya nut, similar to Macadamia.

and upon discovering it
we will find ourselves with your pure image.
Because all your new earth is your 'Little Johnny'
'Little Juan Diego'
'Little wooden steps'
'Ordinary people'
'Leaf'
'String'
'Tail'
'Little Man'
who returning love to You, 'oh, the smallest of your daughters'
—from 'this place whereshe does not walk and where she does
/not stand—
—will sow the joy of your eyes—
in the furrows your troubles plowed like wounds.[7]

---

7.   (Cuadra, <u>Poesia I</u>, 2003, pp. 115-116)

APPENDIX D

Pablo Antonio Cuadra,
Sister Maria and the Devil

by Carlos Mantica

I saw PAC a couple of weeks before he died and on saying goodbye he told me: 'We have much to talk about.' For Pablo talking was a necessity. Now and then he called me and would say to me: 'I need to talk with you...and then it was he who came to my office, in spite of his apparent illness. First he hugged 'Crazy Bird,' as he always called my son, Carlos, for whom he had a special affection, and later sat down to a long talk with me. It was on one of these occasions that he spoke with me about Sister Maria Romero.

'In December of 1972 —he told me— I received in La Prensa a letter from Sister Maria. In it she prophesied that a terrible earthquake was coming very soon upon Managua, in which many people would die and that we should alert the population. I met with Pedro Joaquin to discern what we should do with the letter and both of us were of the opinion to not publish it, because in it Sister Maria complained of the indecent dances, of mini-skirts and of other things that to her eyes gravely offended God, and both Pedro and I thought that the people would laugh at the 'ridiculousness' of the saint, and would mock her, a thing that we wanted to avoid. Her letter was still on my desk on the day of the catastrophe.'

'A few years later I traveled to Costa Rica and wanted to visit Sister Maria. 'You see, little Pablo? You did not pay any attention to me!' were her first words. 'Well, now I warn you of what is coming, an enormous pouring out of blood and this time all over Nicaragua.' Her second prophesy began to be fulfilled in the following months and tens of thousands of Nicaraguans died in an absurd war between brothers that drowned the country in pain and misery.' Without doubt they talked of many more things, perhaps of Granada, his birthplace, certainly of the things of the Lord whom both loved and served. At the end of the visit Sister Maria took Pablo by the hand and told him: 'Come, I want to show you my closet.' She had remodeled with brackets and hangers a very large room where she kept the clothing she collected for her poor.

Upon putting her first foot in the room everything began to tremble and shake. The coat-hangers and clothing fell to the floor, but it was evident to Pablo that it was only the clothing and not the house that trembled. "Oh, no, boy!" then shouted Sister Maria —"Get out of here, I won't put up with you now!...You see, Little Pablo? Every so often it is this same ignorance!" With the first 'Get out of here' the Demon left and the 'show' was over.'

When Pablo told me this he smiled, but I am sure that when it fell to him to be witness of the incident, he was frightened... possibly not so much for the 'idiocy' of that demon, but to see how naturally, with simplicity and authority the saint faced the attacks of the Evil One. From other sources I have learned that what happened with the clothing happened many times. 'Every so often,' as Sister Maria said. Sister Maria...did not give them attention nor importance, because pride is the major sin of demons, and their greatest joy is to be able to be always the center of attention. Sister Maria treated them as she treated an aggravating child.

Carlos Mantica ends his reflection with the following message to PAC: 'Greet Sister Maria for me, and pray much for me and for this your Nicaragua that keeps on counting on you all...and that still is full of demons. Hugs, Chale.'[8]

───────────────

8.   (Mantica, Carlos. ¡Pura Jodarria!, Managua, Hispamer, 2007, pp. 104-105.)

APPENDIX E

Letter to Pablo Antonio Cuadra
about the Giants

by Thomas Merton

At a moment when all the discordant voices of modern society attempt to exorcize the vertigo of man with scientific clichés or prophetic curses, I come to share with you reflections that are neither tragic, nor, I hope, fatuous. They are simply the thoughts of one civilized man to another, dictated by a spirit of sobriety and concern, and with no pretentions to exorcize anything. The vertigo of the twentieth century needs no permission of yours or mine to continue. The tornado has not consulted any of us, and will not do so. This does not mean that we are helpless. It only means that our salvation lies in understanding our exact position, not in flattering ourselves that we have brought the whirlwind into being by ourselves, or that we can calm it with a wave of the hand.

It is certainly true that the storm of history has arisen out of our own hearts. It has sprung unbidden out of the emptiness of technological man. It is the genie he has summoned out of the depths of his own confusion, this complacent sorcerer's apprentice who spends billions on weapons of destruction and space rockets when he cannot provide decent meals, shelter and clothing for two-thirds of the human race. Is it improper to doubt the intelligence and sincerity of modern man? I know it is not accepted as a sign of progressive thinking to question the enlightenment of the twentieth century barbarian. But I no longer have any desire to be considered enlightened, by the standards of the stool pigeons and torturers whose most signal claim to success is that they have built so many extermination camps and operated them to the limit of their capacity.

These glorious characters, reveling in paroxysms of collective paranoia, have now aligned themselves in enormous power blocs of which the most striking feature is that they resemble one another like a pair of twins. I have not clearly understood from Ezekiel that Gog and Magog were to fight one another, although I knew that they were to be overcome. I knew that their ponderous brutality would exhaust itself on the mountains of Israel and provide a feast for the birds of the air. But I had not expected that we would all be so intimately involved in their downfall. The truth is that there is a little of Gog and Magog even in the best of us.

We must be wary of ourselves when the worst that is in man becomes objectified in society, approved, acclaimed, and deified, when hatred becomes patriotism and murder a holy duty, when spying and denunciation are called love of truth and the stool pigeon is a public benefactor, when the gnawing and prurient resentments of frustrated bureaucrats become the conscience of the people and the gangster is enthroned in power, then we must fear the voice of our own heart, even when it denounces them. For are we not all tainted with the same poison?

That is why we must not be deceived by the giants, and by their thunderous denunciations of one another, their preparations for mutual destruction. The fact that they are powerful does not mean that they are sane, and the fact that they speak with intense conviction does not mean that they speak the truth. Nor is their size any proof that they possess a metaphysical solidity. Are they not perhaps specters without essence, emanations from the terrified and puny hearts of politicians, policemen and millionaires?

We live in an age of bad dreams, in which the scientist and the engineer possess the power to give external form to the phantasms of man's unconscious. The bright weapons that sing in the atmosphere, ready to pulverize the cities of the world, are the dreams of giants without a center. Their mathematical evolutions are hieratic rites devised by Shamans without belief. One is permitted to wish their dreams had been less sordid.

But perhaps they are also the emanations of our own subliminal ego!

2

I have learned that an age in which politicians talk about peace is an epoch in which everybody expects war: the great men of the earth would not talk of peace so much if they did not secretly believe it possible, with _one more war_, to annihilate their enemies forever. Always, 'after just one more war,' it will dawn, the new era of love: but first everybody who is hated must be eliminated. For hate, you see, is the mother of their kind of love.

Unfortunately, the love that is to be born out of hate will never be born. Hatred is sterile; it breeds nothing but the image of its own empty fury, its own nothingness. Love cannot come of emptiness. It is full of reality. Hatred destroys the real being of man in fighting the fiction which it calls 'the enemy.' For man is concrete and alive, but 'the enemy' is a subjective abstraction. A society that kills real men in order to deliver itself from the phantasm of a paranoid delusion is already possessed by the demon of destructiveness because it has made itself incapable of love. It refuses, '_a priori_,' to love. It is dedicated not to concrete relationships of man with man, but only to abstractions about politics, economics, psychology, and even, sometimes, religion.

Gog is a lover of power, Magog is absorbed in the cult of money: their idols differ, and indeed their faces seem to be dead set against one another, their madness is the same: they are the two faces of Janus looking inward and dividing with critical fury the polluted sanctuary of dehumanized man.

Only those names matter, to Gog and Magog, only labels, only numbers, symbols, slogans. For the sake of a name, a classification, you can be marched away with your pants off to be shot against a wall. For the sake of a name, a word, you can be gassed in a shower-bath and fed to the furnace to be turned into fertilizer. For the sake of a word or even a number they will tan your skin and make with it into lampshades. If you want to get a job, make a living, have a home to live in, eat in restaurants and ride in vehicles with other human beings, you must have the right classification: depending perhaps on the shape of your nose, the color of your eyes, the kink in your hair, the degree to which you are sunburned, or the social status of your grandfather. Life and death today depend on everything except what you *are*. This is called 'humanism.'

Condemnation or rehabilitation have no connection with what you happen to have done. There is no longer any question of ethical standards. We may have been liberated from the idealistic objectivity about 'right and wrong'. This timely liberation from ethical norms and laws enables us to deal with an ever increasing population of undesirables in much more efficient fashion. Attach to each one an arbitrary label, which requires no action on his part and no effort of thought on the part of the accuser. This enables society to get rid of 'criminals,' without the latter putting anyone to any kind of inconvenience by committing an actual crime. A much more humane and efficient way of dealing with crime! You benevolently shoot a man for all the crimes that he might commit before he a chance to commit them.

3

I write you from Magog's country. The fact that Magog to me is more sympathetic than Gog, does not, I think, affect my objectivity. Nor does it imply a choice of category, a self-classification. Magog and I seldom agree, which is one reason why I write this letter. I must however admit I feel indebted to Magog for allowing me to exist, which Gog perhaps might not. Perhaps it is not to my credit that I half-trust the strain of idealism in Magog, accepting it uncritically as a sign that, for all his blatant, materialistic gigantism, he is still human. Certainly he tolerates in his clients elements of human poignancy, together with an off-beat frivolity which Gog could never comprehend. (Yet Gog, in the right mood, weeps copiously into his vodka). Magog, on the whole, is not demanding. A little lip service has been enough at least up to the present. He does not require the exorbitant public confessions which are a prelude to disappearance in the realm of Gog. The pressure of Magog is more subtle, more gently persuasive, but no less universal. Yet disagreement is still tolerated.

Magog is in confusion, an easier prey than Gog to panic and discouragement. He is less crafty as a politician, and he is handicapped by a vague and uncomplicated system of beliefs which everyone can understand.   Hence the whole world can easily see the discrepancies between his ideals and actualities. Magog is more often embarrassed than Gog, who entertains no objective ideals but only pays homage to a dialectical process by which anything, however disconcerting, can quickly be justified.

Gog, I believe, is fondly hoping that Magog will be driven to despair and ruin himself in some way before it becomes necessary to destroy him. But in any case he is giving Magog every opportunity to discredit himself in the eyes of the rest of the world, so that if he cannot be persuaded to put his own head in the gas oven, his destruction can be made to appear as no crime but as a benefit conferred on the whole human race.

But let me turn from Gog and Magog to the rest of men. And by 'the rest of men' I mean those who have not yet committed themselves to the cause of one or the other of the champions. There are many, even among the power groups, who hate wars and hate the slogans, the systems and the official pronouncements of groups under whose dominance they live. But they seem to be able to do nothing about it. Their instinct to protest is restrained by the awareness that whatever they may say, however true, against one implacable power can be turned to good use by another that is even more inhuman. Even in protest one must be discrete, not only for the sake of protecting one's skin, but above all for the sake of protecting the virginity of one's own protest against the salacious advances of the publicist, the agitator, or the political police.

4

Let me abandon my facetiousness, and consider the question of the world's future, if it has one. Gog and Magog are persuaded that it has: Gog thinks that the self-destruction of Magog will usher in the golden age of peace and love. Magog thinks that if he and Gog can somehow shoot the rapids of a cold war waged with the chemically pure threat of nuclear weapons they will both emerge into a future of happiness, the nature and the possibility of which still remain to be explained.

I for my part believe in the very serious possibility that Gog and Magog may wake up one morning to find that they have burned and blasted each other off the map during the night, and nothing will remain but the spasmodic exercise of automatic weapons still in the throes of what has casually been termed overkill. The superogatory retaliation may quite conceivably affect all the neutrals who have managed to escape the main event, but it is still possible that the southern hemisphere may make a dazed and painful comeback, and discover itself alone in a smaller, emptier, better-radiated but still habitable world.

In this new situation it is conceivable that Indonesia, Latin America, Southern Africa and Australia may find themselves heirs to the opportunities and objectives which Gog and Magog shrugged off with such careless abandon.

The largest, richest and best developed single land-mass south of the Equator is South America. The vast majority of its population is Indian, or of mixed Indian blood. The white minority in South Africa would quite probably disappear. A relic of European stock might survive in Australia and New Zealand. Let us also hopefully assume the partial survival of India and of some Moslem populations in central and northern Africa.

If this should happen it will be an event fraught with a rather extraordinary spiritual significance. It will mean that the more cerebral and mechanistic cultures, those which have tended to live more and more by abstractions and to isolate themselves more and more from the natural world by rationalization, will be succeeded by the sections of the human race which they oppressed and exploited without the slightest appreciation for or understanding for their human reality.

Characteristic of these races is a totally different outlook on life, a spiritual outlook which is not abstract but concrete, not pragmatic but hieratic, intuitive and affective rather than rationalistic and aggressive. The deepest springs of vitality in these races have been sealed up by the Conqueror and Colonizer, where they have not actually been poisoned by him. But if this stone is removed from the spring perhaps its waters will purify themselves by new life and regain their creative, fructifying power. Neither Gog nor Magog can accomplish this for them.

Let me be quite succinct: the greatest sin of the European-Russian-American complex which we call 'the West' (and this sin has spread its own way to China), is not only greed and cruelty, not only moral dishonesty and infidelity to truth, but above all *its unmitigated arrogance towards the rest of the human race.* Western civilization is now in full decline into barbarism (a barbarism that springs *from within itself*) because it has been guilty of a twofold disloyalty: to God and to Man. To a Christian who believes in the mystery of the Incarnation, and who by that belief means something more than a pious theory without real humanistic implications, this is not two disloyalties but one. Since the Word was made Flesh, God is in man. God is in *all men.* All men are to be seen and treated as Christ. Failure to do this, the Lord tells us, involves condemnation for disloyalty to the most fundamental of revealed truths. 'I was thirsty and you gave me not to drink. I was hungry and you gave me not to eat...' (Matthew 25:42). This could be extended in every possible sense: and is meant to be so extended, all over the entire area of human needs, not only for bread, for work, for liberty, for health, but also for truth, for belief, for love, for acceptance, for fellowship and understanding.

One of the great tragedies of the Christian West is the fact that for all the good will of the missionaries and colonizers (they certainly meant well, and behaved humanly, according to their lights which were somewhat brighter than ours), they could not recognize that *the races they conquered were essentially equal to themselves and in some ways superior.*

It was certainly right that Christian Europe should bring Christ to the Indians of Mexico and the Andes, as well as to the Hindus and the Chinese: but where they failed was in their inability to *encounter Christ* already potentially present in the Indians, the Hindus and the Chinese.

Christians have too often forgotten the fact that Christianity found its way into Greek and Roman civilization partly by its spontaneous and creative adaptation of the pre-Christian natural values it found in that civilization. The martyrs rejected all the grossness, the cynicism and falsity of the cult of the state gods which was simply a cult of secular power, but Clement of Alexandria, Justin and Origen believed that Herakleitos and Socrates had been precursors of Christ. They thought that while God had manifested himself to the Jews through the Law and the Prophets he had also spoken to the Gentiles through their philosophers. Christianity made its way in the world of the first century not by imposing Jewish control and social standards on the rest of the world, but by abandoning them, getting free of them so as to be 'all things to all men.' This was the great drama and the supreme lesson of the Apostolic Age. By the end of the Middle Ages that lesson had been *forgotten.* The preachers of the Gospel to newly discovered continents became preachers and disseminators of European culture and power. They did not enter into dialogue with ancient civilizations: they imposed upon them their own monologue and in preaching Christ they also preached themselves. The very ardor of their self-sacrifice and of their humility enabled them to do this with a clean conscience. But they had omitted to listen to the voice of Christ in the unfamiliar accents of the Indian, as Clement had listened for it in the Pre-Socratics. And now, today, we have a Christianity of Magog.

It is a Christianity of money, of action, of passive crowds, an electronic Christianity of loudspeakers and parades. Magog is himself without belief, cynically tolerant of the athletic yet sentimental Christ devised by some of his clients, because this Christ is profitable to Magog. He is a progressive Christ who does not protest against Pharisees or money changers in the temple. He protests only against Gog.

It is my belief that we should not be too sure of having found Christ in ourselves until we have found him also in the part of humanity that is most remote from our own.

Christ is found not in loud and pompous declarations but in humble and fraternal dialogue. He is found less in a truth that is imposed than in a truth that is shared.

5

If I insist on giving you my truth, and never stop to receive your truth in return, then there can be no truth between us. Christ is present 'where two or three are gathered in my name.' But to be gathered in the name of Christ is to be gathered in the name of the Word made flesh, of God made man. It is therefore to be gathered in the faith that God has become man and can be seen in man, that he can speak in man and that he can enlighten and inspire love in and through any man I meet. It is true that the visible Church alone has the official mission to sanctify and teach all nations, but no man knows that the stranger he meets coming out of the forest in a new country is not already an invisible member of Christ and perhaps one who has some providential or prophetic message to utter.

Whatever India may have had to say to the West she was forced to remain silent. Whatever China had to say, though some of the first missionaries heard it and understood it, the message was generally ignored as irrelevant. Did anyone pay attention to the voices of the Maya and the Inca, who had deep things to say? By and large their witness was merely suppressed. No one considered that the children of the Sun might, after all, hold in their hearts a spiritual secret. On the contrary, abstract discussions were engaged in to determine whether, in terms of academic philosophy, the Indian was to be considered a rational animal. One shudders at the voice of cerebral Western arrogance even then eviscerated by the rationalism that is ours today, judging the living spiritual mystery of primitive man and condemning it to exclusion from the category on which love, friendship, respect, and communion were made to depend.

God speaks, and God is to be heard, not only on Sinai, not only in my own heart, but in the *voice of the stranger.* That is why the peoples of the Orient, and all primitive peoples in general, make so much of the mystery of hospitality.

God must be allowed the right to speak unpredictably. The Holy Spirit, the very voice of Divine Liberty, must always be like the wind in 'blowing where he pleases.' (John 3:8) In the mystery of the Old Testament there was already a tension between the Law and the Prophets. In the New Testament the Spirit himself is Law, and he is everywhere. He certainly inspires and protects the visible

Church, but if we cannot see him unexpectedly in the stranger and the alien, we will not understanding him even in the Church. We must find him in our enemy, or we may lose him even in our friend. We must find him in the pagan or we will lose him in our own selves, substituting for his living presence an empty abstraction. How can we reveal to others what we cannot discover in them ourselves? We must, then, see the truth in the stranger, and the truth we see must be a newly living truth, not just a projection of a dead conventional idea of our own – a projection of our own self upon the stranger.

The desecration, de-sacramentalization of the modern world is manifest above all by the fact that the stranger is of no account. As soon as he is 'displaced' he is completely unacceptable. He fits into no familiar category, he is unexplained and therefore a threat to complacency. Everything not easy to account for must be wiped out, and mystery must be wiped out with it. An alien presence interferes with the superficial and faked clarity of our own rationalizations.

6

There is more than one way of morally liquidating the 'stranger' and the 'alien.' It is sufficient to destroy, in some way, that in him which is different and disconcerting. By pressure, persuasion, or force one can impose on him one's own ideas and attitudes towards life. One can indoctrinate him, brainwash him. He is no longer different. He has been reduced to conformity with one's own outlook. Gog, who does nothing if not thoroughly, believes in the thorough liquidation of differences, and the reduction of everyone else to a carbon copy of himself. Magog is somewhat more quixotic: the stranger becomes part of his own screen of fantasies, part of the collective dream life which is manufactured for him on Madison Avenue and in Hollywood. For all practical purposes, the stranger no longer exists. He is not even seen. He is replaced by a fantastic image. What is seen and approved, in a vague, superficial way, is the stereotype that has been created by the travel agency.

This accounts for the spurious cosmopolitanism of the naïve tourist and travelling business man, who wanders everywhere with his camera, his exposure meter, his spectacles, his sun glasses, his binoculars, and though gazing around him in all directions never sees what is there. He is not capable of doing so. He is too docile to his instructors, to those who have told him everything beforehand. He believes the advertisements of the travel agent at whose suggestion he bought the ticket that landed him wherever he may be. He has been told what he was going to see, and he thinks he is seeing it. Or, failing that, he at least wonders why he is not seeing what he has been led to expect. Under no circumstances does it occur to him to become interested in what is actually there. Still less to enter into a fully human rapport with the human beings who are before him. He has not, of course, questioned their status as rational animals, as the scholastically trained colonists of an earlier age might have done. It just does not occur to him that they might have a life, a spirit, a thought, a culture of their own which has its own peculiar individual character.

He does not know why he is travelling in the first place: indeed he is travelling at somebody else's suggestion. Even at home he is alien from himself. He is doubly alienated when he is out of his own atmosphere. He cannot possibly realize that the stranger has something very valuable, something irreplaceable to give him: something that can never be bought with money, never estimated by publicists, never exploited by political agitators: the spiritual understanding of a friend who belongs to a different culture. The tourist lacks nothing except brothers. For him these do not exist.

The tourist never meets anyone, never encounters anyone, never finds the brother in the stranger. This is his tragedy, and it has been the tragedy of Gog and Magog, especially of Magog, in every part of the world.

If only North Americans had realized, after a hundred and fifty years, that Latin Americans really existed. That they were really people. That they spoke a different language. That they had a culture. That they had more than something to sell! Money has totally corrupted the brotherhood that should have united all the peoples of America. It has destroyed the sense of relationship, the spiritual community that had already begun to flourish in the years of Bolivar. But no! Most North Americans still don't know, and don't care, that Brazil speaks a language other than Spanish, that all Latin Americans do not live for the siesta, that all do not spend their days and nights playing the guitar and making love. They have never awakened to the fact that Latin America is by and large culturally superior to the United States, not only on the level of the wealthy minority which has absorbed more of the sophistication of Europe, but also among the desperately poor indigenous cultures, some of which are rooted in a past that has never yet been surpassed on this continent.

So the tourist drinks tequila, and thinks it is no good, and waits for the fiesta he has been told to wait for. How should he realize that the Indian who walks down the street with half a house on his head and a hole in his pants, is Christ? All the tourist thinks is that it is odd for so many Indians to be called Jesus.

7

So much for the modern scene: I am no prophet, no one is, for now we have learned to get along without prophets. But I would say that if Gog and Magog are to destroy one another, which they seem quite anxious to do, it would be a great pity if the survivors in the 'Third World' attempted to reproduce their collective alienation, horror and insanity, and thus build up another corrupt world to be destroyed by another war. To the whole third world I would say there is one lesson to be learned from the present situation, one lesson of the greatest urgency: be unlike the giants, Gog and Magog. Mark what they do, and act differently. Mark their official pronouncements, their ideologies, and without any difficulty you will find them hollow. Mark their behavior: their bluster, their violence, their blandishments, their hypocrisy: by their fruits you shall know them. In all their boastfulness they have become the victims of their own terror, which is nothing but the emptiness of their own hearts. They claim to be humanists, they claim to know and love man. They have come to liberate man, they say. But they do not know what man is. They are themselves less human than their fathers were, less articulate, less sensitive, less profound, less capable of genuine concern. They are turning into giant insects. Their societies are becoming anthills, without purpose, without meaning, without spirit and joy.

What is wrong with their humanism? It is a humanism of termites, because without God man becomes an insect, a worm in the wood, and even if he can fly, so what? There are flying ants. Even if man flies all over the universe, he is still nothing but a flying ant until he recovers a human center and a human spirit in the depth of his own being.

Karl Marx? Yes, he was a humanist, with a humanist's concerns. He understood the roots of alienation and his understanding even had something spiritual about it. Marx unconsciously built his system on a basically religious pattern, on the Messianism of the Old Testament, and in his own myth Marx was Moses. He understood something of the meaning of liberation, because, he had in his bones the typology of Exodus. To say that he built a 'scientific' thought on a foundation of religious symbolism is not to say that he was wrong, but to justify what was basically right about his analysis. Marx did not think only with the top of his head, or reason on the surface of his intelligence. He did not simply verbalize or dogmatize as his followers have done. He was still human. And they?

Ultimately there is no humanism without God. Marx thought that humanism had to be atheistic, and this was because he did not understand God any better than the self-complacent formalists whom he criticized. He thought, as they did, that God was an idea, an abstract essence, forming part of an intellectual superstructure built to justify economic alienation. There is in God nothing abstract. He is not a static entity, an object of thought, a pure essence. The dynamism Marx looked for in history was something that the Bible itself would lead us in some sense to understand and to expect. And liberation from religious alienation was the central theme of the New Testament. But the theme has not been understood. It has too often been forgotten. Yet it is the very heart of the mystery of the Cross.

8

It is not with resignation that I wait for whatever may come, but with an acceptance and an understanding which cannot be confirmed within the limits of pragmatic realism. However meaningless Gog and Magog may be in themselves, the cataclysm

308 PABLO ANTONIO CUADRA

they will undoubtedly let loose is full of meaning, full of light. Out of their negation and terror comes certitude and peace for anyone who can fight his way free of their confusion. The worst they can do is bring death upon us and death is of little consequence. Destruction of the body cannot touch the deepest center of life.

When will the bombs fall? Who shall say? Perhaps Gog and Magog have yet to perfect their policies and their weapons. Perhaps they want to do a neat and masterly job, dropping 'clean' bombs, without fallout. It sounds clinical to the point of humanitarian kindness. It is all a lovely, humane piece of surgery. Prompt, efficacious, sterile, pure. That of course was the ideal of the Nazis who conducted the extermination camps twenty years ago: but of course they had not progressed as far as we have. They devoted themselves dutifully to a disgusting job which could never be performed under perfect clinical conditions. Yet they did their best. Gog and Magog will develop the whole thing to its ultimate refinement. I hear they are working on a bomb that will destroy nothing but life. Men, animals, birds, perhaps also vegetation. But it will leave buildings, factories, railways, natural resources. Only one further step, and the weapon will be one of absolute perfection. It should destroy books, works of art, musical instruments, toys, tools and gardens, but not destroy flags, weapons, gallows, electric chairs, gas chambers, instruments of torture or plenty of strait jackets in case someone should accidentally survive. Then the era of love can finally begin. Atheistic humanism can take over.

APPENDIX F

A remembrance of Thomas Merton

by Pablo Antonio Cuadra

In the state of blue grasses, farmer and gentleman, leaving behind the ranches of millionaires and the meadows of white corrals of the 'pure blood,' when the gentlemen landowners are no longer called 'Coronels' and rustic houses of old wood can be seen, clothes hanging on the line, poverty and unkempt forests, still further on —changing the old bus in a small town and helping oneself to a rental car driven by a lady— among the pines.

I think of the mountains of Kentucky upon which snow falls at mid-afternoon, where the cry of the strange birds increases the silence of the forests, in which the crack of the of the monks' axe was everlasting and mine in which I could see solitude grow until I felt free...

There, in a bend in the road the high wall encloses Peace. The Abbey of Gethsemane (The Trappists, say the country folk, 'those Trappists'), will this be the house whose nostalgia men from the Bluegrass State have sung about for centuries: 'My old Kentucky home'...? 'We are going to sing a song in honor of the old Kentucky home, the old Kentucky home, far, far away...'

We say peace, we seek peace. They say it pointing with machine guns or intimidating their spooked birds with devastating bombs. Or placing their frightened dove against the firing squad walls. Here, over the entryway it says: PAX INTRANTIBUS. Whosoever would know that which is true, authentic peace, that which does not deceive: enter!

I went to find the great Trappist poet and I found him training in the school of Peace. Fed, nourished, made peace. Thomas Merton was first a white habit that entered in the night, silently opening the door of the cell where I was being housed. He hugged me: 'Peace be with you.' Then I saw his face: ingenuous, diaphanous, but where the dynamic fever that besieged the factions of men from the North had dissipated, and the smile —all the face is smile— can only be described as beatitude. That is to say: eyes that return from contemplation and not from business; muscles of the countenance only occupied in loving; ears resting within the silence and the Trappist song. Beatitude. He is not an angel that has come down to earth. He is a man whose sufferings, concerns and anguish, have been slowly softened, passing his hand daily and softly over his hairy skin and now wolves and serpents obey, they enter my cell with him, domesticated but recognizable. Merton is real, of the here and now, all that we know he carries with him, but all has been overcome. He is not an angel. He is a soldier who returns from the war, a businessman who returns from his exhausting sales, a philosopher who returns from his anguish, a poor man who returns from his hunger, all that pains us is in his face, but remade by love: he is the confessor of our life, its witness.

But he gives testimony of Peace. 'Our monasteries are schools of love,' —he tell me. We conversed long that night while the moon illuminated the reddish leaves of a beautiful tree that lifted a beggar branch toward my window. (Then was also there, with his white habit, Ernesto Cardenal.) Merton has an infinite curiosity about Hispanic-America: he listened, read poems, looked at photographs. A strange eagerness for the destiny of this new world in whose eyes, years ago, upon entering a temple, read for the first time the inescapable presence of God.

'We have a tremendous and marvelous vocation,' – he tell me; 'the vocation to be Americans. That is to say, to be and to form the true America ('Christian-America'), that of Christ who carried America in a mysterious Advent, the crucified Christ upon the Cross who forms the dew and the encounter of this double continent and who agonizes over her. One day he will come resurrected in the unity and in the liberty of 'the new men.' We must be prophets of his Advent, like Pasternak has been in Russia. We must form a union of creators, of thinkers, of men of prayer, a union without any more organization than charity…'

His voice is soft, convincing, of an internal enthusiasm that flows and exalts the level of his waters without accentuating his voice. He spoke of Pasternak. He was one of his friends. His correspondence flies to all latitudes like a dovecote whose courses are blown by the Holy Spirit himself. Besides this, he works incessantly —poems, essays, articles and various books each year. I am united with him like I am with you all,'— he tells me about Pasternak. (Later Pasternak was witness, a martyr of that Advent. He had premonition about Russia as a poet. He sang and suffered persecution because of the prophesy). And he insisted about America: 'We have an enormous debt to the Indians. His religious feeling is Christian property and a spiritual wealth that we must not lose.' He dreams about having a branch of the Trappist Order that would flourish in Latin-America, imbibing religious meaning and the common life of the Indian. Trappists in 'tunics' going out from the farms and huts toward a new American conception of what is human and what is life.

Because Merton is a man horrified by the dehumanization of modern life. He was its victim. He felt all the weight of anguish until after climbing and falling seven times in the path of the mountain of seven circles, he found the door of Peace: PAX INTRANTIBUS.

'Sometimes I think that only the Psalms, the Prophets of the Bible and Job, are able to articulate our anguish in an adequate manner. All of humanity climbs inexorably to Calvary with the Lord like the repentant thief or like the other; or —something worse— like the Pharisees. All climb. Here the pain jumps the roofs of the monastery, we share the anguish.' And he adds: 'In our refectory, instead of the lives of saints, many times we read diaries, letters, reports of political prisoners or of concentration camps. We must be very united one to the other —where there is someone suffering there is a brother— very united in humility and poverty and fortitude. United also with the poor of history, like the poets of the Psalms, like the Indian poets. All are Christ. We have to know it and be witnesses of the Truth and of the Mystery.'

Merton rejoices greatly hearing the Spanish language. To him it is especially beloved. He believes that his poems gain something by passing to Spanish. Ernesto reads a translation of the poem 'Advent' by Merton:

Bewitched with cleanliness these nights of Advent, oh holy
                                                  /spheres,
while the minds, gentle like animals,
Reunite under the roof among the sweet hay;
And the intellects are more silent than the flocks that graze
                                                  / under the stars.
Oh, overturn your darkness and your clarity in our solemn
                                                  /valleys
Oh heavens: and travel like the beautiful Virgin,
Toward the majestic sunset of the planets,
Oh white full moon as silent as Bethlehem!

During the day we walk the fields of the monastery. The tractors break the earth with their noisy plows. The axes cut firewood at the edges of the forest. All the monks work in silence. When we pass they bow in silence and greet us with a smile, as though the Archangels were woodsmen. They are almost all young men, full of vitality and fortitude. Later I will see them in the chorus. Or in the dining hall in the frugal food of fruit of the earth. No meat. Only cereals. Not one word. When they want something, they talk with their hands, with slight signs, moving the air in an inaudible poem. And they smile, they are full of joy and peace.

The monk's life is a farmer's life and a poet's life: they work the earth and work their mind: read, study, sing. At mid-night the chorus gets up and sings the Psalms within the shadows. It is a spectacle that astounds: the poems of the Bible in grave voices anticipating the song of the birds. A hard life, rustic, manly. At sun-down they go to bed. And the Masses are before dawn. And when the brothers open their arms to greet with the Peace of Christ, the roosters rattle the stained glass and the dawn makes thousands of little birds twitter. I never saw faces more pure —never saw a look so certain of God— like that of the brother when he showed me the host and invited me to receive it: 'This is the body of Our Lord Jesus Christ.'

Later, at nine, is the Great Mass sung by all. When it was over I went with Merton along the edge of a small lake where pines and aspens are reflected. He spoke to me of poetry (no one had told me such things): of poetry as a divine function. We are the birds of the Ark of the Covenant. Those called to sing of the gifts of God. Those that are sent to seek the olive and return to the hands of the Father with the testimony of the earth. Poetry is prayer.

In the afternoon I walk through the monastery: the library where the monks read in silence; the dormitories —the hard beds in a row, a coarse mat for bed—; the cloisters with their Way of the Cross remembering the painful and divine road; the barns; and in a garden full of joy, the cemetery of the monks: crosses without name. The monk has no biography. He is anonymous as the people of God. 'The dormitory,' Merton calls it. There they await the future awakening.

I remember there Thomas Merton, conversing, speaking of life upon the earth, of anonymity and of death. There he collects for me his perenniality. To him was conceded the Word, but as a custodian, like a shepherd of those silences he has sung:

> *Brothers, the curved plants and their daughters*
> *will never publish your elegies:*
> *our brothers trees, in summer garb,*
> *keep vigil over our fame in these green cradles:*
> *The simple crosses are content*
> *To hide your identities.*[9]

9.　(Cuadra, <u>Critica literaria II</u>. 2004, pp. 213-217.)

BIBLIOGRAPHY

Alcina Franch, J. (189-2008). *Mitos y literatura azteca.* Madrid: Alianza Editorial, S.A.

Arellano, J. E. (1997 segunda edición). *Pablo Antonio Cuadra: Aproximaciones a su Vida y Obra:* . Managua: Academia Nicaragüense de la Lengua; Editorial Ciencias Sociales, INIES.

Argüello Lacayo, J. (2000). *Un Pobre de Jesús.* Managua: Hispamer.

Bochen, C. M. (1993). *Thomas Merton: The Courage for Truth: Letters to Writers.* San Diego, New York, London: Harcourt Brace & Company.

Cardenal, E. (2004 2nd Edition). *La Revolucion Perdida.* Managua: anama Ediciones Centroamericanas.

Cardenal, E., & Salmon, R. O.-g. (1992). *Los Ovnis de Oro: Golden UFO's.* Bloomington and Indianapolis: Indiana University Press.

Cohen, Jonathan: Translator. (1984, 2nd edition 1985). *Ernesto Cardenal: With Walker in Nicaragua and Other Early Poems 1949-1954.* Middletown, CT: Wesleyan University Press.

Cuadra, P.A. (2004). *Crítica Literaria II.* A Remebrance of thomas Merton. Managua: Colección Cultural de Centro América.

Cuadra, P. A. (1993; 13th edition 2004). *El Nicaragüense.* Managua: Hispamer.

Cuadra, P. A. (2003). *Ensayos II;.* Managua: Colección Cultural de Central América; editado por Pedro Xavier Solís Cuadra.

Cuadra, P. A. (1966). personal letter. (G. Guardia, Entrevistador)

Cuadra, P. A. (2003). *Poesía I.* Managua: Colección Cultural de Centro América.

Cuadra, P. A. (2003). *Poesía II.* Managua: Colección Cultural de Centro América; editor Pedro Xavier Solís Cuadra.

Elizondo, V. (2007). *Jesús de Galilea: Un Dios de Increibles Sorpresas.* Chicago: Loyola Press.

Gargiullo, M. B., Magnuson, B., & Kimball, L. (2008). *A Field Guide to Plants of Costa Rica.* New York: Oxford University Press.

Garibay K., A. M. (1992). *Historia de la Literatura Nahuatl.* México: Editorial Porrua.

Garrigues, R., & Dean, R. (2007). *The Birds of Costa Rica.* Ithaca, New York: A Zona Tropical Publication; Cornell University Press.

Guardia, G. (2004, 2007). Pablo Antonio Cuadra: Poeta y Pensador Cristiano (Ensayo). *Cistercium Revista Cisterciense del Centro Internacional de Estudios Misticos, Editorial Promesa.*

Kühl, E. (2000). *Matagalpa y Sus Gentes.* Managua: Publicaciones y Servicios Nicaragua Fácil.

Lacayo, J. A. (2000). *Un Pobre de Jesús.* Managua: Hispamer.

Lacayo, J. A. (2000). *Un Pobre de Jesús: Padre Azarías H. Pallais.* Managua: Hispamer.

Mántica A., C. (2007). *!Pura Jodarria!: Nicaragua en Broma y en Serio.* Managua: Hispamer.

Rafaela Herrera. (n.d.). *Wikipedia* .

Salas Estrada, D. J. (2002). *Biogeografía de Nicaragua.* Managua: INAFOR.

Solís Cuadra, P. X. (2008). *Pablo Antonio Cuadra: Itinerario.* Managua: Academia Nicaragüense de la Lengua; PAVSA.

Solís Cuadra, P. X. (1996). *Pablo Antonio Cuadra: Itinerary.* Managua: Hispamer.

Solís, P. X. (2001). *El Movimiento de Vanguardia de Nicaragua.* Managua: Colección Cultural de Centro América, Serie Literaria, 11.

The New Open Bible Study Edition. (1990). *New American Standard Bible.* Nashville, Tennessee: Thomas Nelson Publishers.

White, S. F. (2002). *El Mundo Más Que Humano en la Poesía de Pablo Antonio Cuadra: Un Estudio Ecocrítico.* Managua: Asociación Pablo Antonio Cuadra; Multimpresos Nicaragüenses.

White, S. F., & Arellano, J. E. (1988). *Pablo Antonio Cuadra: The Birth of the Sun: Introduction to the Poetry of Pablo Antonio Cuadra.* Greensboro, NC: Unicorn Press.

White, S., & Simon, G. T. (2007). *Seven Trees Against the Dying Light: Pablo Antonio Cuadra.* Evanston, Illinois: Northwestern University Press.

Wieck, R. S. (1988). *Time Sanctified: The Book of Hours in Medieval Art and Life.* New York: Braziller.

Woodward, R. L. (2005). The Imperial Ghost of WIlliam Walker. *H-Net Reviews in the Humanities and Social Sciences* , 1-4.

Ximénez, F. F. (2005). *Popul Vuh, versión de Agustín Estrada Monroy.* México: Editores Mexicanos Unidos, S.A.

Yepes Boscan, G. (1996). The Religious Poetry of Pablo Antonio Cuadra. En P. A. Cuadra, *Book of Hours* (págs. vii-ix). Caracas: FUNDARTE.

SPANISH LANGUAGE EDITIONS

I) **Essays and Criticism**

Conny Palacios: *Pluralidad de máscaras en la lírica de Pablo Antonio Cuadra*.

Eduardo Zepeda-Henríquez: *Linaje de la poesía nicaragüense*.

Julio Ycaza Tigerino: *La cultura hispánica y la crisis de Occidente*.

Jorge Eduardo Arellano: *Pablo Antonio Cuadra / Aproximaciones a su vida y obra*.

Guillermo Rothschuh Tablada: *Las uvas están verdes*.

Günther Schmigalle: *"Dichoso el asno que es apenas comprensivo"*. *Ge Erre Ene y sus parodias de Rubén Darío*.

Pedro Xavier Solís: *Vida de papel*.

Guillermo Rothschuh Tablada: *Mitos y mitotes*.

Erick Aguirre: *Las máscaras del texto / Proceso histórico y dominación cultural en Centroamérica*.

Plutarco Cortez: *Posmodernidad y pensamiento ágil*.

Addis Esparta Díaz Cárcamo: *Existencialismo y metafísica en la poesía de Alfonso Cortés*.

II) **Nature**

Octavio Robleto: *El buscador de paisajes*.

III) **Tributes**

Varios: *Neruda en la garganta pastoril de América*.

Varios: *Pablo Antonio Cuadra en la Academia*.

Varios: *Memorial de José Jirón Terán / vida y obra.*

Varios: *Premio "Doctor Carlos Martínez" al Doctor Carlos Tünnermann Bernheim.*

IV) **Speeches of Initiation in the Academy**

José Jirón Terán: *Los prólogos de Rubén Darío: Vasos comúnicantes de las letras españolas e hispanoamericanas.*

Carlos Tünnermann Bernheim: *La paideia en Rubén Darío.*

Julio Valle-Castillo: *Las humanidades en la poesía nicaragüense.* (En coedición con el CNE).

V) **Lexicons and Linguistics**

Fernando Silva: *La lengua de Nicaragua / Pequeño diccionario analítico.*

Enrique Peña-Hernández: *Refranero zoológico popular.* [2.ª edición].

Fernando Silva: *La lengua de Nicaragua / Pequeño diccionario analítico.* [2.ª ed. aumentada con dos apéndices].

Comisión de Lexicografía y Gramática: *Diccionario de Uso del Español Nicaragüense.*

Róger Matus Lazo: *Cómo hablan los adolescentes en Nicaragua.*

Fernando Silva: *La lengua nuestra de cada día.*

Enrique Peña-Hernández: *Refranero zoológico popular.* [3.ª edición].

Jorge Eduardo Arellano: *Del idioma español en Nicaragua (glosas e indagaciones).*

Francisco Arellano Oviedo: *Diccionario del español de Nicaragua.* (marzo, 2007).

Francisco Arellano Oviedo: *Diccionario del español de Nicaragua.* [3.ª edición, aumenta y corregida, noviembre, 2007].

Auxiliadora Rosales Solís: *Atlas lingüístico de Nicaragua: nivel fonético.*

VI)   Series: Ruben Dario

Varios: *Rubén Darío en la Academia.*

Rubén Darío: *España contemporánea* / Edición crítica de Noel Rivas Bravo.

José Jirón Terán: *Por los caminos de Rubén Darío.*

Rubén Darío: *Cartas desconocidas* / Compilación general: José Jirón Terán; introducción, selección y notas: Jorge Eduardo Arellano.

Rubén Darío: *Teatros.* La tournée de Sarah Bernhardt en Chile (1886). Edición de Ricardo Llopesa.

Günther Schmigalle: *La pluma es arma hermosa* / Rubén Darío en Costa Rica.

Rubén Darío: *Don Quijote no debe ni puede morir* / Prólogo de Jorge Eduardo Arellano, anotaciones de Günther Schmigalle.

José Jirón Terán: *Rubén Darío visto por Juan de Dios Vanegas.*

José Jirón Terán: *Prólogos de Rubén Darío.*

Varios: *Repertorio dariano 2010.*

Jorge Luis Castillo: *Gris en azul: el tedio y la creación poética en Rubén Darío y la lírica hispanoamericana posmodernista (Lugones, Pezoa Véliz, Luis Carlos López).*

Rubén Darío: *Crónicas desconocidas.* Edición, introducción y notas de Günther Schmigalle.

Ignacio Campos Ruiz: *Ficcionalización (auto)biográfica de Rubén Darío en la novela centroamericana: entre la construcción mítica y su deconstrucción.*

Rubén Darío: *La república de Panamá y otras crónicas desconocidas.*

Varios: *Repertorio dariano 2011-2012.*

VII)   Original Creations

Pablo Antonio Cuadra: *Exilios* (poemas).

Enrique Peña-Hernández: *Al pie del Coyotepe* (relatos y crónicas).

Francisco Arellano Oviedo: *Monumentum aere perennius.* (Poemas).

Pablo Antonio Cuadra: *El Nicán Náuat.*

Fernando Silva: *Versos son.*

Eduardo Zepeda-Henríquez: *Amor del tiempo venidero.*

El "Grupo U" de Boaco: Antología poética y labor teatral / Flavio Tigerino, Armando Íncer y otros. (En coedición con la Embajada de España en Nicaragua y el INCH).

Carlos Alemán Ocampo: *Aventuras de Juan Parado, señor de El Diriá.* (Relatos).

Jorge Eduardo Arellano: *La camisa férrea de mil puntas cruentas.*

Fernando Silva: *Son cuentos.*

Minificciones de Nicaragua. Prólogo, Selección y Notas de Jorge Eduardo Arellano.

Guillermo Rothschuh Tablada: *Tela de cóndores* / Homenaje a Oswaldo Guayasamín.

Fernando Silva: *Uno dice cosas.* (Poesía).

Álvaro Urtecho: *Tierra sin tiempo.* (Poesía).

Fernando Silva: *9 cuentos.* (Cuentos).

Guillermo Menocal Gómez: *Recopilación temporal. (Relacortos, prosemas y comentarios).*

Salomón de la Selva: *Tropical Town and Other Poems* / *Ciudad tropical y otros poemas.*

Guillermo Menocal Gómez: *Selección poética.*

Rosario Aguilar: *Miraflores.*

Pablo Antonio Cuadra: *Book of hours.* English Translation: Sarah Hornsby and Matthew C. Hornsby

VIII) Nicaraguan History

Pía Falk y Louise Fribert: *La estatuaria aborigen de Nicaragua.*

Carlos Mántica Abaunza: *El Cuecuence o el gran sinvergüenza.*

Fernando Silva: *La historia natural de El Güegüence.*

Clemente Guido Martínez: *Los dioses vencidos de Zapatera: mitos y realidades.*

Jorge Eduardo Arellano: *El beisbol en Nicaragua: rescate histórico y cultural (1889-1948).*

IX) **Biography**

Jorge Eduardo Arellano: *El sabio Debayle y su contribución a la ciencia médica en Centroamérica.*

Pedro Xavier Solís: *Pablo Antonio Cuadra / Itinerario.*

Isolda Rodríguez Rosales: *Me queda la palabra...*